A Nation and its Navy at War

Edition 2

Ranjit B. Rai

Copyright © 2015 Ranjit B. Rai
ISBN 13: 978-81-930055-8-3 ISBN 10: 81-930055-8-9
All rights reserved.

Published by

Frontier India Technology
No 22, 4th Floor, MK Joshi Building, Devi Chowk, Shastri Nagar,
Dombivli West, Maharashtra, India. 421202
http://frontierindia.org
https://www.facebook.com/frontierindiapublishing
The views expressed in this book are those of the author and not at all of the publisher. The publisher is not responsible for the views of the author and authenticity of the data, in any way whatsoever. Cataloging / listing of this book for re-sale purpose can be done, only by the authorised companies. Cataloging /listing or sale by unauthorized distributors / bookshops /booksellers etc., is strictly prohibited and will be legally prosecuted. All disputes are subject to Thane, Maharashtra jurisdiction only.

DEDICATION

Dedicated To My Family Who Navigate this Navigator
And To The Fine Indian Navy That I Served.
The Nation Will Need Its Strength In The Future
And History of 1971 War Will Give Succor.

CONTENTS

	Acknowledgments	I
1	Preface	1
2	Prologue	3
3	Dramatis Personae	17
4	The Order of Battle - India and Pakistan	27
5	Naval Orbat - India 1971	31
6	Naval Orbat - Pakistan 1971	35
7	The Mukti Bahini's civil War	37
8	America's Anti India Tilt	43
9	The Pre-War Period (Sep - Nov 1971)	52
10	Day by Day Account of the War	66
11	The Sinking of PNS Ghazi	97
12	INS Khukri goes down	102
13	The story of Ashok Roy VRC and Roy Choudhry	108
14	The surrender	112
15	Causes of Pakistani defeat	120
16	Pakistan navy at War (Maj. Gen. Fazal Muqueem Khan)	124
17	Epilogue : The Future	136

ACKNOWLEDGMENTS

It was August 1985. After almost four full years in challenging but enjoyable sea-going assignments including an eventful command, I found myself perched on the top floor of the Navy Office building (Noorbhoy House) in Bombay as an Officer on Special Duty (OSD). I was awaiting an appointment order that emanates from New Delhi. It was the height of the monsoon. A state of inertia followed.
Vice Admiral S. Mookerjee, PVSM, AVSM, the then Flag Officer Commanding-in-Chief Western Naval Command asked me in his inimitable way to swiftly and completely rewrite the Western Naval Command Orders (WENCO) into three volumes—for posterity, he remarked. He added that in my spare time I was free to pursue any other professional work.
Having read Elmo Zumwalt's On Watch, Kissinger's White House Years and Nixon's Memoirs I had always been encouraged to study Kissinger, by that prodigious America watcher, the learned Mr. N.K. Bhojwani. So I began to pen my thoughts, when Commander Uday Bhaskar the Naval P.R. man in Delhi rand down and request me to do a few articles for Navy Week 85. From all this ennui emerged masses of ink spilt on paper, and this modest book.
Acknowledgements are therefore due to many. Mrs. Seema Sengar the Librarian from British Council who made available materials from various archives. The library staff of St. Xavier's College, SNDT, and Command Reference Library INS Angre (for old issues of naval magazines) were most helpful. Thanks go to leading newspapers who gave me access to 1971 clippings. Encouragement from Arvind Dabir and Ravi Sikka was always forthcoming. Professional extracts from Jane's 1971, that invaluable lexicon of naval ships by Capt J.E. Moore is deeply acknowledged.
Acknowledgements are most certainly due to those at home who bore reams of paper, Praveena, Raul and Ritin. They invariably helped but said, 'I'd never complete the book, more as a challenge than anything else. Mr. G.B. Pai however, with two books to his credit always said where there's a will a way will be found.
Typing chores devolved upon Leading Writer R. Singh and Shri. Chitnis. They got so enthused with this simple work of naval history that they worked with me on many a Saturday, thanks to the five-day. They so enjoyed the cups of tea and samosas (stand easy) I religiously served every time five pages were faired.
Acknowledgements are due to the officers in Naval Headquarters and Ministry of Defence who perused the manuscript and offered much valuable advice for final publication.
I also acknowledge Lancer International for publishing this book in 1987 and permission to reprint.

PREFACE

A concatenation of circumstances found India at war with Pakistan for 14 days in 1971 and in this conflict of implication, the Indian Navy played a major role and demonstrated its power and potential with glory, both in its inventiveness and the gallantry and bravery of its officers and men. This book seeks to chronicle those events as viewed by the media and as explained by the Naval personnel who took party in the action.

The elections of December 1970 had given a clear mandate to the Awami League of East Pakistan which won a majority of seats in the Pakistan Assembly. To thwart the democratic vote and the surge for greater autonomy for East Pakistan, the rulers of West Pakistan launched a process of suppression and reprisals there with the help of the Army which included the arrest of Sheikh Mujibur Rahman. The Army brutalities resulted in a gargantuan influx of refugees into the eastern states of India. India could not be indifferent to the influx, which reached the alarming proportions of about eight million souls.

The rebel activities of the Mukti Bahini and the skirmishes by the armed forces of Pakistan on India's border made the war inevitable. All appeals by the Indian Prime Minister to the nations of the world for a political settlement proved futile and the cry in East Pakistan became one for full autonomy.

In all this, one can clearly discern the 'tilt' of USA towards Pakistan inspired, among other things, by the Nixon Administration's pronounced differences with Indian policy and the desire to forge a new relationship with China through the agency of Pakistan. This aspect of the time has been touched upon with due regard to the concerned American personalities who have now published their revelations and possibly deserve comment.

The narration of events, complied from available and unclassified contemporary documents may have serious gaps which in matters of war can be filled only when the official record is ultimately unclassified and made public. Even so, from what is known and well authenticated, 1971 was a year of stirring deeds worth recording for posterity and not to be consigned to the limbo of oblivion.

The Indian Navy, ever since it acquired its own entity in 1947, came to grips with reality for the first time in 1971 when it fought side by side with its sister Services to secure the ultimate defeat of the enemy. In the earlier skirmishes and wars with Pakistan and China, the role of the Navy was more of a bystander for action, when necessary. The brunt of the action was borne by the Army and Air Force. In the 1971 war, with maritime problems on hand, the fighting took place both on land and the high seas.

Under the inspired guidance of the Chief of the Indian Navy, Admiral S.M. Nanda, the Naval forces were enthused into accomplishing significant victories beyond the call of duty and the realms of what seemed possible. This book is mainly dedicated to the extraordinary actions of India's Silent Service during the 1971 war jointly with the sister Services.

This, then, is a story of the Indian Navy at war; of its achievements, and losses, and violent actions in its first major trial as it were. The old tars not only came off well with flying, or shall we say, sailing colours, with their decorations of Vir Chakras and Maha Vir Chakras but also with widows and fatherless children, who albeit are now forgotten, for well was it written:

> "God and a Soldier and people adore
> In time of War, not before;
> And when war is over and all things are righted
> God is neglected and an old Soldier slighted."

I am grateful to those who took the trouble to speak about actions in which they were involved and lent me their time to speak about their experiences of the courage of the finest officers and sailors of this proud Service in 1971 that faced the powder and inspired me to write. I have stuck to facts, yet some omissions are unavoidable. A Naval officer attempting authorship for the first time, I have tried to convey the spirit and the flash of the Navy in the 1971 war. This alone has been the objective.

With changes in maritime strategy and the scramble for the seas, facing the enemy will not be a new thing for the Indian Navy. A tradition of competence and confidence has b now been well established and I hope younger generations of the Navy will look back upon 1971 with a sense of pride, inspiration and challenge.

Rightfully, Navy Day is now celebrated nationally on 4 December, commemorating the Indian Navy's first daring attack on Karachi in 1971. It is also a day for the nation to ponder over its maritime force and in return, for the Service to reaffirm its loyalty and dedication to the defence of the nation. This book is so dedicated.

The views expressed in this book are my own and do not reflect those of the Indian Navy or the Government of India.

RANJIT B. RAI
Bombay
23 December 1985

PROLOGUE

The British were adept at the rules of the colonial game for survive they did, by the theory of divide and quit, time and again Britannia created two Pakistan's East and West, seemingly the same. But separated them by a thousand leagues of Indian terrain Never the two could meet.

Relations, between India and Pakistan have always been strained, and marked by a blow-hot blow-cold approach and mutual distrust. The erstwhile British rulers created Pakistan in two segments in 1947 over 1000 miles apart. The people of West Pakistan comprising Sindhi, Balochi and Punjabi Muslims had only one feature in common with the people of East Pakistan -religion. In their cultural heritage, language, physical environment, economic resources, temperament and history, no two people could be more unlike each other. There was no place for mutual empathy between them, no sense of common caring and sharing. These differences were accentuated by the fact that the seat of political power in Pakistan lay in power as a matter of right. The people of West Pakistan exercised political power as a matter of right. The people of East Pakistan appeared to be taken for granted. When democracy yielded place to dictatorship the alienation between the two became more permanent. East Pakistan also failed to produce any leader of stature save Maulana Bhashani, and later Sheikh Mujibur Rahman, a protégé of Suhrawardy, even though the Awami League was formed in 1949. The rapid succession of leaders in Pakistan following the death of Mohammed Ali Jinnah is noteworthy. Nawabzada Liaquat Ali Khan assassinated in 1951; Khwaja Nazimkuddin Khan (1951-53) (dismissed); two Mohammed Alis, Suhrawardy (1956) and then came Chundrigar in 1957 for 55 days. The last in the line of civilian leaders was Malik Feroze Khan Noon (1957 to 7 Oct 1958) a quiet, polished, well read, and an accomplished gentleman. In what was to become a new breed of military rulers, he was thrown out of office in 1958 by Mohammed Ayub Khan, a general with good tastes in wine and women, and links with the famous Christine Keeler too. Nepotism and corruption took roots in the polity of Pakistan till one day, on 29 March 1969, the General abdicated in favour of General Yahya Khan. It was during this leader's tenure that the scene for "Bangladesh" was set.

Interestingly, ever since the day in 1948 when Jinnah visited the Dacca University to impose Urdu as the lingua franca of Pakistan and was heckled the indications till 1971 were that East Pakistan would not easily accept West Pakistan's chauvinism or heavy handedness in this matter. Resentment to the superior attitude shown by the military rulers of West

Pakistan was always evident. Yet despite pestilence, floods and series of Governors who adroitly ruled East Pakistan, the people weathered the storms, political or otherwise. Intrigues by rulers and even supported by the famous anti-Indian American, John Foster Dulles who acclaimed Pakistan as the bulwark of freedom in Asia kept both Pakistan's moving as one. The feelings of East Pakistanis were well summed up by a right-wing leader in the Constituent Assembly when he said:

"Sir, I actually stated yesterday and said that the attitude of the Muslim League was of contempt towards East Bengal, towards its culture, its language, its literature and everything concerning East Bengal. In fact, Sir, I tell you that far from considering East Bengal as an equal partner the leaders of the Muslim League thought that we were a subject race and they belonged to a race of conquerors." (Quoted in Keith Callard, Pakistan—A Political Study, London, 1957)

The statistics of trade, jobs, revenue and spending given in the chart below amply illustrate that East Pakistan was dominated by a minority in West Pakistan. Though both states of Pakistan were Muslim, there were basic ethnic differences. The 78 million Bengalis have a different language from the 58 million West Pakistanis. The westerners are all, light skinned, rugged and generally healthy and hardened, inhabiting a large expanse of arid land, while the easterners are small, dark skinned, soft natured people with a lush tropical and richer land. Yet more resources were allocated to the West than to the East and here lay short of chasm—a gap between the two Pakistan's designed as it were by the British and accepted by the people of the subcontinent in the quest for freedom. It had to come to a divide a one day.

SOME ECONOMIC INDICATORS

	East Pakistan	West Pakistan
Area (in square miles)	54,501	310,236
Population (1970 estimate)	70 Million	60 Million
Five-year plan allocation		
1st	32%	68%
2nd	32%	68%
3rd	36%	64%
4th (unlikely to be implemented)	52%	47.5%
Foreign aid allocation	20-30%	70-80%
Export earning	50-70%	30-50%
Import expenditure	25-30%	70-75%
Industrial assets owned	11%	

by Bengalis		
Civil service jobs	16-20%	80-84%
Military jobs	10%	90%
Resources transferred from East to West between 1948-49 and 1968-69	Rs. 31,120 million	
Per capita income, official		
1964-65	Rs. 285.5	Rs. 419.0
1968-69	Rs. 291.5	Rs. 473.4
Regional difference in p.c.i., Official		
1959-60	32%	
1964-65	47%	
1968-69	62%	
Real difference in p.c.i., 1968-69	95%	
Real difference in average Standard of living, 1968-69	126%	
Proportion of income spent on Food by industrial workers (1955-56 survey)	69-75%	60-63%

*At the official rate, US $1=4.76 rupees (RS.) cultural market exchange rate, $1=Rs. 11).

EDUCATIONAL DISPARITIES

	East Pakistan		West Pakistan	
	1947	1967	1947	1967
Primary level				
Number of institutions	29,633	28,255	8,413	33,271
Number of students	2,020,000	4,310,000	550,000	2,740,000
Secondary level				
Institutions	3,481	4,390	2,598	4,563
Students	53,000	107,000	51,000	153,000
General College				
Institutions	50	173	40	239
Enrolment	19,000	138,000	13,000	142,000
General University				
Institutions	1	2	2	4
Enrolment	1,600	8,000	700	10,000

Foreign Trade Statistics (Rs. In Thousands)

	East Pakistan		West Pakistan	
	Exports	Imports	Exports	Imports
1947-53	4,581,596	2,128,628	3,785,806	4,768,923
1952-57	3,969,766	2,159,552	3,440,371	5,105,093
1957-62	5,508,335	3,831,924	2,724,169	8,554,170
1962-67	6,922,694	7,063,692	5,754,368	15,960,025
Grand Total 1947-67	20,982,391	15,123,796	15,704,714	34,388,211

Earlier (in 1986) Mujibur Rahman had been under trial in West Pakistan for his role in the famous Agartala conspiracy case but when released he had returned to East Pakistan as a hero. Now he was the most popular leader and the champion of the people's aspirations. Yet he was being denied his right to be the leader of Pakistan.

The elections held on 7 December 1970 were peaceful but they brought about a sea-change in East Pakistan. As the Dacca-based Pakistan Observer commented: "We made it, we did it. The era of people's rule has begun. We are entering from darkness into light." It appeared as if he the Bengalis despite their chasm had reached their goal and for having a fair election the hatred against the West subsided and disappeared. However, as President Yahya Khan delayed the convening of the National Assembly, the happy and hopeful atmosphere was fading. The fact that during his visit to Dacca in January 1971, Yahya Khan agreed to convene the Assembly on 6 February 1971 and again delayed it to merely a meeting to be convened on 3 March 1971, made it clear that the President was on the horns of a dilemma.

As coincidence would have it, on 30 January 1971 two young Kashmiris hijacked an Indian Airlines Fokker Friendship plane from Srinagar to Lahore and blew it up there. India remonstrated against Pakistan's complicity in the episode and stopped all Pakistani overflights. Thus at a time when free movement was essential to the two Pakistan's a sense of isolation was created, which was termed as an Indian plot. The chasm of distance and immobility was added to the other divisions between the two Pakistan's.

The situation in East Pakistan was deteriorating fast. Both Admiral S.M. Ahsan, the Governor, and Lt Gen Sahabzada M. Yaqub Khan recommended a political solution, but Gen Yahya Khan, impelled by Zulfikar Ali Bhutto, had other plans and he clamped down reprisals on 25 March 1971.

Now emerged Col M.A.G. Osmany, a retired East Bengal Regiment Officer who made contingency plans for acquiring power by political means and if that failed by force and in the end to seek India's help. Sensing the mood of the military, he planned what was later to be the Mukti Bahini.

Foreign Policy and Politics

Since the 1962 Chinese aggression when Nehru's "Hindi-Chini, Bhai-Bhai" philosophy was shattered and India lost ground to China over the McMahon Line, and the 1965 operations when tracts of India came under Pakistan occupation, the sphere of India's foreign policy was governed and influenced by Pakistan and China. This is t rue even today. Tensions in relations with Pakistan were obvious at the conference of Muslim countries held at Rabat in 1970. The national liberation movement in East Pakistan began gaining ground; its growing influence culminated in the victory of the Bengali national party, the Awami League (people's League), in the election held on 7 December 1970. The results of the election were not acceptable to the ruling junta in West Pakistan and they rejected the mandate, dispersed the legislature bodies in East Pakistan and arrested Sheikh Mujibur Rahman. An armed repression by the Pakistani Army against the Bengali supporters of a democratic movement was let loose on 25 March 1971, resulting in mass destruction and killings for the next eight months which led to some eight million refugees, mainly Hindus and Bihari Muslims fleeing to India across the border. The feeding and rehabilitation of such large numbers placed a heavy burden on the Indian economy. The chasm between East and West Pakistan widened and India was at the receiving end. Sheikh Mujibur Rahman was accused of treason and committed to trial by court martial. The Bengalis now smarting, jobless, bitter and filled with hate, were ready for a long struggle demanding nothing short of autonomy within Pakistan. India looked to the world to redress this chasm before it grew wider. Inexplicably, the response of many democratic foreign nations, notably the USA, failed to give much redress or weightage to the passions that were unleashed in East Pakistan. Military aid to Pakistan continued and no diplomatic leverage of sanctions to get Yahya Khan to come to a political settlement of East Pakistan emerged. The American tilt to Pakistan is discussed more extensively in Chapter Four. In the event, between March and November 1971 a war of fanatic fury with barbaric acts of rape, loot, plunder, arson and murder was unleashed upon the Bengalis by the Pakistani Army. The Razakars (informants) seemed to inflame the Army further to go on these rampages. Whenever army patrols emerged from alleys after killing unarmed Bengalis they came out gleefully shouting—"Narai Takbir" (Victory for God) and "Pakistan Zindabad" (Long live Pakistan).

When Mujibur Rahman called for a non-cooperation movement in early March, he was tricked by Yahya Khan. The deceiving General flew in troop enforcements to the East and on 15 March landed in Dacca himself with a smoke-screen approach to negotiate. On 23 March Mujib flew a new flag—the green, red and yellow banner of Bangladesh—from his home whilst negotiations with Yahya Khan were in progress. It was the red rag to the bull. By now, a friend of Yahya, Gen Tikka Khan who had earned for himself the sobriquet of 'Butcher of Baluchistan' had emerged on the sense. His earlier indiscriminate air and artillery strikes against Balochi's to repress a tribal revolt had earned for him this notoriety. He made his lists of 'suspects'—professors, doctors, community leaders and businessmen—all of whom were dragged away by army squads never to be seen again.

Foreign Policy and Politics

Since the 1962 Chinese aggression when Nehru's "Hindi-Chini, Bhai-Bhai" philosophy was shattered and India lost ground to China over the McMahon Line, and the 1965 operations when tracts of India came under Pakistan occupation, the sphere of India's foreign policy was governed and influenced by Pakistan and China. This is t rue even today. Tensions in relations with Pakistan were obvious at the conference of Muslim countries held at Rabat in 1970. The national liberation movement in East Pakistan began gaining ground; its growing influence culminated in the victory of the Bengali national party, the Awami League (people's League), in the election held on 7 December 1970. The results of the election were not acceptable to the ruling junta in West Pakistan and they rejected the mandate, dispersed the legislature bodies in East Pakistan and arrested Sheikh Mujibur Rahman. An armed repression by the Pakistani Army against the Bengali supporters of a democratic movement was let loose on 25 March 1971, resulting in mass destruction and killings for the next eight months which led to some eight million refugees, mainly Hindus and Bihari Muslims fleeing to India across the border. The feeding and rehabilitation of such large numbers placed a heavy burden on the Indian economy. The chasm between East and West Pakistan widened and India was at the receiving end. Sheikh Mujibur Rahman was accused of treason and committed to trial by court martial. The Bengalis now smarting, jobless, bitter and filled with hate, were ready for a long struggle demanding nothing short of autonomy within Pakistan. India looked to the world to redress this chasm before it grew wider. Inexplicably, the response of many democratic foreign nations, notably the USA, failed to give much redress or weightage to the passions that were unleashed in East Pakistan. Military aid to Pakistan continued and no diplomatic leverage of sanctions to get Yahya Khan to come to a political settlement of East Pakistan emerged. The American tilt to Pakistan is discussed more extensively in Chapter Four. In the event, between March and November 1971 a war of fanatic fury with barbaric acts of rape, loot, plunder, arson and murder was unleashed upon the Bengalis by the Pakistani Army. The Razakars (informants) seemed to inflame the Army further to go on these rampages. Whenever army patrols emerged from alleys after killing unarmed Bengalis they came out gleefully shouting—"Narai Takbir" (Victory for God) and "Pakistan Zindabad" (Long live Pakistan).

When Mujibur Rahman called for a non-cooperation movement in early March, he was tricked by Yahya Khan. The deceiving General flew in troop enforcements to the East and on 15 March landed in Dacca himself with a smoke-screen approach to negotiate. On 23 March Mujib flew a new flag—the green, red and yellow banner of Bangladesh—from his home whilst negotiations with Yahya Khan were in progress. It was the red rag to the bull. By now, a friend of Yahya, Gen Tikka Khan who had earned for himself the sobriquet of 'Butcher of Baluchistan' had emerged on the sence. His earlier indiscriminate air and artillery strikes against Baluchis to repress a tribal revolt had earned for him this notoriety. He made his lists of 'suspects'—professors, doctors, community leaders and businessmen—all of whom were dragged away by army squads never to be seen again.

India's Predicament

April saw anger grow in India over the helplessness and groans of refugees and the burden of demands to provide food and rehabilitation to the incoming millions. Why should India pick up the bill for Pakistan's atrocities was an oft asked question. Aid from USA and UK in food, equipment and cash which ran into over $100 million did come India's way but the cost of maintaining and caring for eight million refugees could well run into over a billion dollars a year if not halted or the conditions improved. Pressure on Mrs. Gandhi to use military force mounted. But the fear of China was there and she resisted and tolerated the onrush, hopeful of an amicable diplomatic settlement on the refugee issue. Little did she know then that the USA was biased and her appeals would be of no avail. There were doves as well as hawks in Pakistan; it is now known that two Major Generals, Umer Khan, Chairman of the National Security Council and Mohammed Akbar, Chief of inter-services intelligence and Rizvi of Central Intelligence expressed serious partisan misgivings posing as hawks on the issue. Mrs. Gandhi toured abroad for a last-ditch to resolve the refugee problem.

Mrs. Gandhi's Role and Response

Mrs. Gandhi appealed to heads of state throughout the world asking them to solve the problem of refugees and turbulence in East Bengal, which were essentially of Pakistan's making. Her appeal was directed to the USA particularly with a request to stop her arms aid to Pakistan. Failing in eliciting an appropriate response and on learning that Henry Kissinger secretly visited Peking via Rawalpindi in early July to arrange Nixon's visit to China, Mrs. Gandhi also suspected that a Washington-Islamabad-Peking alliance was in the offing. She lost no time in signing on 9 August 1971 the 20-year treaty with Moscow which included steps for cooperation, Peace and collaboration, clause 9 of which reads as follows:

"In the event of an attack or a threat thereof the two (India and USSR) would immediately enter into mutual consultations in order to remove such threat and to take appropriate effective measures to ensure the peace and security of their countries."

This surprised many for it seemed incompatible with the concept of non-alignment, but his measure was possibly prompted by the fear of Chinese-US collusion and what the refugee influx would do to the stability and economy of the country if not halted. Mrs. Gandhi's fears and her diplomatic scoop to sign this treaty did put India deeper into USSR's hands militarily but the lady seemed to have foreseen the rebuff from USA and China. It is possible this tactic prevented the Chinese and the USA from any direct action later in December. Nixon did send his task force led by USS Enterprise but it did not take up any active role. In October Mrs Gandhi after a visit to USSR, made a last-ditch attempt to tour Western countries to seek a peaceful solution to the refugee problem and the call for autonomy in East Pakistan. Her tour report filed by Keesing's Archives is recounted for the light it throws on the amount of effort she made to obtain a political settlement.

Mrs. Gandhi left New Delhi on Oct. 24 for a tour of six Western capitals, her first stop being Brussels, where she began talks on the following day with the Belgian Prime Minister, Gaston Eyskens.

At a press conference on Oct. 26 Mrs. Gandhi said that there was no basis for negotiations between India and Pakistan on Bangladesh and continued: "the present situation has arisen because of something which happened in East Bengal, and we are suffering because of that. We are not directly involved in it. So something has to be done first to settle that problem." Asked whether India would repatriate the refugees forcibly if international support was not forthcoming, she replied: "I cannot say what India will do, because one has to see what the situation is at the given moment and take decisions. I am clear in my mind that we are not willing to absorb these refugees in our country."

Mrs. Gandhi flew on Oct. 28 that India was not agreeable to the U.N. sending observers to supervise the withdrawal of troops from the borders, and asked: "Why was the U.N. not interested when there were only Pakistani forces deployed along the frontier, and only became concerned when Indian troops were involved?" Pakistan, she declared, had committed "a major crime" in which over 1,000,000 people had died. Whilst reiterating India's determination to see that the refugees returned, she said that it was unrealistic to expect them to go back while atrocities continued in East

Bengal. In a television interview on the same day she said that India would have to consider recognizing an independent Bangladesh if that would contribute towards a solution. The chances of a political settlement were less than before, she added, as the elected representatives of East Bengal had been locked up and replaced by appointed deputies from splinter groups which had received hardly any votes at the last elections.

Mrs. Gandhi arrived in London on Oct. 29, and spent Oct. 30-31 at Chequers, where she had confidential talks with the Prime Minister, Mr. Ted heath. She afterwards told journalists that she was "on the whole satisfied" with the talks. She met Sir Alec Douglas-Home at the Foreign Office on Nov. 1, and visited Oxford on the following day, where she received the honorary degree of Doctor of Civil Law.

Addressing a public meeting in London on Oct. 31, Mrs. Gandhi said: "Ever since the Pakistan Government launched its actions of brutality in East Bengal, ever since the refugees started pouring into India as a result of it, we tried our best to make other countries realize the gravity of the situation. Yet nobody did anything about it. And when our security was threatened and we had to move our troops as a precaution, suddenly we were given advice that we should accept U.N. observers on the border or that the troops of both countries should be withdrawn for the border. Thus once again India was equated with Pakistan, although the situation was entirely a Pakistani creation and although Pakistan's actions had threatened our security." She emphasized that India was not basically opposed to the idea of U.N. observers, pointing out that there were already 10 observers of the U.N. High Commission for Refugees in India who were free to go anywhere, and continued: "We do not want the destruction of Pakistan or the destruction of her integrity. At the same time we do not want our freedom or our interests to be threatened, and we are determined to protect them with our strength."

The Indian Prime Minister told a press conference on Nov. 1 that some 30,000 refugees daily—and on one day 62,000—were still coming across the border when she left India. There were 2,50,000 Muslims, the rest being Hindus, Christians or of other religions. "We are absolutely determined that the vast majority must go back," she declared. "We are not going to tolerate them on our soil." The Pakistan Government's action had forced them out, and it was up to Pakistan to create conditions for their safe return.

Mrs. Gandhi flew to Washington on Nov. 4 for talks with President Nixon. After their meeting the White House stated that the President supported the withdrawal of troops from the frontiers by both sides.

Speaking at a dinner at the White House on the same day Mrs. Gandhi again referred to the magnitude of the refugee problem, and continued: "Imagine the entire population of Michigan State suddenly converging on

New York State, and imaging the strain it would cause on the Administration and on services such as health and communications and on resources like food and money—this not in conditions of affluence, but in a country already battling with problems of poverty and huge population ... From those who value democratic principles we expect understanding and, may I add, a certain measure of support ... Our people cannot understand how those who are victims and who are bearing a burden and have restrained themselves with such fortitude should be equated with those whose actions has caused the tragedy ..."

Mrs. Gandhi paid a visit to Paris on Nov. 7-10, during which she had talks with President Pompidou and the French Premier, M. Chaban-Delmas. She also received M. Andre Malraux, the distinguished novelist and former Minister of Cultural Affairs, who had stated on Sept. 17 that he had offered to serve with the Mukti Bahini. (M. Malraux served with the Republican Air Force in the Spanish Civil War and commanded the Resistance movement in Alsace Lorraine during the Second World War.)

In a television interview on Nov. 8 Mrs. Gandhi said that she was prepared to meet President Yahya Khan to discuss all the problems between India and Pakistan, but that East Bengal was "not a problem between India and Pakistan but between West Pakistan and the Bengalis". It is perhaps inevitable today that Bangladesh should become independent", she added, "but I do not think that East Bengal would wish to be associated with West Bengal, as the latter is industrialized and would be the dominant partner."

Mrs. Gandhi concluded her tour by visiting Bonn on Nov. 10-13 for talks with Herr Brandt, the West German Chancellor. A statement issued by Herr Brandt on Nov. 11, after expressing the hope that it would be possible to avoid a military confrontation, said that the Federal Government was "ready to support, to the best of its ability, all measures which would help in promoting a political solution of the problem", and was convinced that "a political solution of the problem of East Pakistan must be found that will eliminate the existing situation of strife and ultimately enable the refugees to return home." He also announced that the Federal Government would make a further contribution of DM 50,000,000 ($14,000,000 at the official rate of exchange) towards the relief of the refugees.

Mrs. Gandhi said at a press conference on Nov. 12 that the Indian Government had to give the Mukti Bahini a "minimum of aid" because the Indian people, especially in West Bengal, demanded this, and also because it was unable to prevent them from using Indian territory for recruitment and training, as the frontier was too long for effective control."

After returning to India on Nov. 13, Mrs. Gandhi said in identical statements to both Houses of Parliament on Nov. 15 that she thought that international opinion had shifted from a "tragic indifference" to a growing sense of the urgency of seeking a political solution of the of the Bangladesh issue with the elected leaders. Most countries also realized that the release of Sheikh Mujibur Rahman was essential, and intended to impress this fact on the Pakistani military regime. She had been told of the U.S. decision to stop all further arms shipments to Pakistan and had been given the impression that arms were not being supplied from British, French or West German sources.

This then was the most trying period for the indirectly. It was in this shrewd politician's interest that Mujibur's rise backed by public mandate be stifled. Outwardly in Dacca, Bhutto had referred to Mujib as the future Prime Minister of Pakistan, but when autonomy was demanded by the East Pakistanis, Bhutto sided with the generals to suppress the East and buy time for a West Pakistani coalition government. He played a double-dealing game with his generals, siding one and befriending the other for which later he himself paid a heavy price. Bhutto also visited Peking from 5 to 8 November for consultations with Pakistan's Chinese allies. On arrival, talks were held with Chou En-Lai. Much importance is attached to this visit in the final escalation of attack by the Pakistan Air Force on Indian airfields. There appears to have been some tacit understanding between the Pakistanis and Chinese to give diplomatic support in the United Nations to the quelling of the uprising in East Bengal, to supply arms and possibly to intervene in the event of war. This fact has now been revealed by Henry Kissinger. The non-compliance of the Chinese, when the crunch came, is attributed to a misunderstanding, fear of USSR, and doubt on the part of the Chinese. It could also have been that Bhutto misrepresented the facts to his military leaders. India could not rule out an attack from the north. Generals Manekshaw and Aurora feared this but were prepared for it. They had apprised the Defence Minister, hence had possibly recommended the December period for any action in Bangladesh, as the winter would be at its height, snow would begin to fall thus preventing the Chinese from any large-scale activity—which may well have been the case. A story datelined 13 August 1985 by the Press Trust of India is reproduced after describing Bhutto's visit to China as reported by Keesing's. This was Bhutto's connection and the China-US factor in the 1971 War.

MR. BHUTTO'S VISIT TO PEKING

A Pakistani delegation led by Mr. Z.A Bhutto, the Chairman of the Pakistan People's Party, visited Peking for consultations on 5-8 November. The delegation, which included Mr. S.M. Khan (Foreign Secretary), Air Marshal A. Rahim Khan (C-in-C of the Air Force), Lieut-General Gul Hassan (Army Chief of Staff) and Rear Admiral Rashid Ahmed (Naval,

Chief of Staff), began talks with the Chinese Premier, Mr. Chou En-Lai, immediately after its arrival. At a banquet in honour of the Pakistan delegation the Chinese acting Foreign Minister, Mr. Chi Peng-fei, said on Nov. 7:

"The Indian Government has crudely interfered in Pakistan's internal affairs and carried out subversive activities and military threats against Pakistan by continuing to exploit the East Pakistan question... The East Pakistan question is the internal affair of Pakistani people themselves, and it is absolutely unpermissible for any foreign country to carry out interference and subversion under any pretexts... We believe that the broad masses of the Pakistani people are patriotic, want to safeguard national unity and the unification of the country, and oppose internal splits and outside interference... The reasonable proposal put forward recently by President Yahya Khan for the armed forces of India and Pakistan to withdraw from the border and disengage is helpful to the easing of tension in the subcontinent and should be welcomed.

Out Pakistani friends may rest assured that should Pakistan be subjected to foreign aggression the Chinese Government and people will, as always, resolutely support the Pakistan Government and people in their struggle to defend their State sovereignty and national independence."

Mr. Bhutto refused at a press conference on November 7 to answer question on whether the visit had resulted in promises of increased Chinese military aid for Pakistan, and explained the fact that no joint communiqué was issued at the conclusion of the talks by saying that the two sides had not found the need for one. On returning to Islamabad the following day he said that the mission had been a complete success, and that "concrete and tangible" results had been achieved.

When the refugee question was discussed in the Social, Humanitarian and Cultural Committee of the U.N. General Assembly on November 19 the Chinese representative, Mr. Fu Hao, asserted that "the so-called question of refugees from East Pakistan came into being and developed in the present state because of a certain country's intervention in Pakistan's internal affairs ... These tactics of interference in the internal affairs of other countries are well known to the Chinese Government and people. In our experience, a certain neighbouring country plotted rebellion in the Tibetan region of our country and carried out subversive activities. When the rebellion it plotted, was smashed by the Chinese people, it coerced tens of thousands of Chinese inhabitants into going to its country, creating a question of so-called 'Tibetan refugees' ..."

In hindsight, the recent statements made by Henry Kissinger give tell-tale evidence to the events.

Washington 13 August 1985 (PTI)

The former U.S. National Security Adviser, Dr. Henry Kissinger, disclosed that it was going to intervene on behalf of Pakistan against India during the Bangladesh War, the U.S. would have told Beijing that Washington would not be indifferent to a Soviet attack on China

This message was, however, not delivered because the expected Chinese message conveying the decision to intervene in the war did not come up. In an interview to the Washington Post on Sunday, Dr. Kissinger said the U.S. received word at the height of the war from the Chinese that they would have an important message to deliver a few hours later in the day.

Expecting that this message would be the decision to intervene, the then President, Mr. Richard Nixon, and Dr. Kissinger instructed the Chief of Staff, General Alexander Haig to receive the message and then convey to the Chinese the U.S. assurance to move against the Soviet Union.

The Washington Post questioned Dr. Kissinger about President Nixon's disclosure that during his presidency he considered the use of nuclear weapons four times including once during the Bangladesh war if China intervened on Pakistan's side and the Soviet Union reacted by intervening on behalf of India.

Dr. Kissinger said it was possible that Mr. Nixon in his own mind was prepared to use nuclear weapons in the event of a Soviet intervention on India's side but that issue was never considered by the administration "as a Government".

Post: It appeared at a certain point (in the Indo-Pakistan war) that the Soviets were encouraging the Indians to go on, having mastered East Pakistan and to take West Pakistan also and to disintegrate Pakistan basically. You wrote in your memories that the United States "would not stand idly by", would render significant assistance, the precise nature to be worked out when the circumstances arose.

Kissinger: We believed we had intelligence information that after having defeated East Pakistan, the Indians would attack West Pakistan. Now, we had a special concern with Pakistan at the time because Pakistan had opened China for us and President Nixon was going to China about two months after this crisis developed. Moreover, previous Presidents had made certain commitments about the territorial integrity of Pakistan.

Post: In late November, early December 1971.

Kissinger: But the specific events to which you referred occurred one Sunday morning early in December. President Nixon, General Haig and I were meeting in his office. We received word about 10 O'clock from the Chinese—I could be off but this is generally correct—that they had an urgent message to deliver to us at 2. We thought that the message might be that they would come to the assistance of Pakistan.

We asked General Haig to receive the message and we instructed him to tell the Chinese that, if their decision was to assist Pakistan, we would not be indifferent to a Soviet attack on China. The reaction would have to be worked out in the circumstance that arose. In the event, the Chinese decided not to act.

Had there been a Soviet attack on China, it is highly probable that we would have given assistance to China. The assistance would have had to depend on staff planning that never took place. It is possible that President Nixon in his own mind was prepared to use nuclear weapons, but I think it is important to understand that as a government there was never any discussion of the use of nuclear weapons. Even at that meeting there was no discussion on use of nuclear weapons.

More recently, Pakistan has released parts of the Hamoodur Rehman report. As UNI reported:

Former chief of army staff General Tikka Khan has stated that the reason why he withheld the publication of the Hamoodur Rehman Commission Report on the disintegration of East Pakistan was because it contained a top secret plan of Pakistan Army.

However, after certain modifications had been made in the report, he had been made in the report, he had given clearance for its publication, he clarified.

Even today there is controversy over Mr. Bhutto's role during the 1970 elections, when it is believed he had opposed transfer of power to late Sheikh Mujibur Rahman after his party emerged as the majority party in the erstwhile East Pakistan.

DRAMATIS PERSONAE

The plays the thing.
                              Shakespeare—Hamlet, Act II, Sc 2.

Late MRS INDIRA GANDHI
Prime Minister. Priyadarshini to friends.

She was Prime Minister during 1971, the Indo-Pak War. Her pivotal role is comparable to that of the legendary Winston Churchill. She was clear that the objective of the armed forces was "to help liberate Bangladesh at any cost, hold West Pakistan at bay and, if possible, give it a telling blow, to ensure that it never seeks war again." She set these goals after failing to get a diplomatic settlement for the refugee problem. The morning briefings by General Manekshaw and her approval of action for the day, in concert with Defence Minister Jagjivan Ram, enabled victory. Her failure was to release 93,000 POWS in the Simla Agreement with nothing in return. She was honoured with the highest national award, the Bharat Ratna.

Late Shri JAGJIVAN RAM
Defence Minister. Jaggu Babu to friends.

His astute brain, administrative capabilities, total commitment to the Prime Minister's objectives, and motivated handling of the Service Chiefs, came to the fore during this brief war. He delegated authority for financial and autonomous actions during the war and eliminated bureaucratic delays. He got along with Finance Minister, Y.B. Chavan, and Foreign Minister, Swaran Singh. He fell out with Mrs. Gandhi later and joined the opposition.

Late General S.H.F.J. MANEKSHAW
Later Field Marshal. Chief of Army Staff. Sam Bahadur to friends.

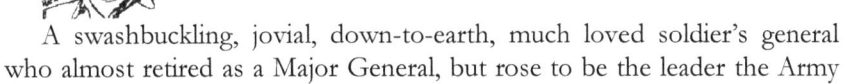

A swashbuckling, jovial, down-to-earth, much loved soldier's general who almost retired as a Major General, but rose to be the leader the Army needed in 1971. His self-assumed role as spokesman for the Navy and the Air Force during high level briefings was like a Chief of Defence Staff. His ability to resolve inter-Service issues at his level spoke well of his leadership. He looked his men in the eye and boosted Army morale no end. A Parsi, he lived like a Gorkha—the regiment that nurtured him and looked after him in his retirement. To them, he was willing to give his all. Awarded Padma Vibhushan.

Late Admiral S.M. NANDA
Chief of Naval Staff. Charles to his friends.

A shrewd manager of men and resources, and a Captain's ideal Admiral. He masterminded clear-cut operational orders, which when read by his lower Commanders and Captains at sea, left no room for doubt. His vision of the Navy's objectives ensured that the Navy came out with flying colours. He saw to it that Manekshaw and Lal gave this small Service a chance. He overruled nervous views to implant his bolder ones. "No risk, no gain" was his motto. His knowledge of Karachi, wide experience in command of INS Mysore, Western Fleet and Command, and as Vice-Chief made him most suited for the post. Adm. Gorshkov the old sea-dog of Russia, was an admirer. Awarded Padma Vibhushan.

Late Air Chief Marshal P.C. LAL
Chief of Air Staff. PC to Friends

This serious soft-spoken intellectual, an ace pilot, applied modern management to take the Indian Air Force to levels of efficiency never attained before. Losses did not deter him from supporting the Navy in its Karachi raids. He worked closely with the other two Chiefs against many odds, in the war which the Indian Air Force faced with distinction. Awarded Padma Vibhushan.

Late Vice Admiral SURENDRA NATH KOHLI
Flag Officer Commanding-in-Chief West. Known as Takarmar Kohli.

Later Admiral, Chief of Naval Staff 1973-1976.

As a Captain, his ship suffered a hat-trick of collisions but he came out unscathed to be given Western Naval Command in 1971. Guided by his Chief during the war, each day saw him take bolder stances and greater responsibility for action in the Western theatre. The loss of Khukri saddened him immensely and he spent many pensive hours wondering how he could have avoided this catastrophe. He dedicated Sea Power and the Indian Ocean to those who lost their lives in the Indian Navy's 1971 actions. Awarded Padma Vibhushan.

Late Vice Admiral N. KRISHNAN
Flag Officer Commanding-in-Chief (East). Tubby Krish to friends. Later Chairman, Cochin Shipyard.

Rotund, sharp-talking and truly brilliant, Krishnan commanded INS Delhi in the 1960 Goa Operations and INS Vikrant with grit. Brain power and command of the language helped him formulate the Indian Navy's plans and his brilliant deployment of INS Vikrant speaks volumes for his tactical foresight. A forceful personality some found difficult to get along with. Awarded Padma Bhushan.

Rear Admiral V.A. KAMATH (Retired)
Flag Officer Commanding South. Vasu to friends. Later Vice Admiral, Vice Chief of Naval Staff

A pipe-smoking, quiet and tradition-conscious officer. He commanded the Southern Naval Area and carried out his functions without much fuss. Awarded PVSM

Late Rear Admiral E.C. KURUVILLA
Later Vice Admiral. Chandy to friends. Chairman and Managing Director, Mazagon Docks Ltd.

A six-feet-two, broad-shouldered Admiral with specialist gunnery training from HMS Excellent. A brawny Admiral who rode horses and drove ships hard. With command experience of INS Kistna, INS Trishul and INS Vikrant, he leaned a lot on his pride and his operational staff when confronted with the intricacies of war at sea and paid scant regard to advice from shore. Awarded PVSM

Late Rear Admiral SRIHARI LAL SARMA
Flag Officer Commanding - Eastern Fleet. Shri to friends. Eastern Fleet Commander formed in October

1971. Hailing from Orissa, a stocky officer with experience and Command of INS Mysore. Spoke with caution and encouraged originality in others. He was ideally suited to be Fleet Commander and obeyed instructions faithfully and well. Was greatly assisted by Captain Suraj Prakash Flag Captain. Awarded PVSM.

Captain R.K.S. GHANDHI
Later Vice Admiral, retired. Russi to friends. Chairman SCI.

A Whale Island trained officer at HMS Excellent and also Flag Lieutenant to Admiral Mountbatten, who had commanded INS Cauvery, Betwa and Trishul with seagoing élan. He was Kuruvilla's Flag Captain in Command of Mysore. Two Gunnery heads, the Flag Captain and Cdr G.M.

Hiranandani, another gunnery specialist, as Fleet Operations Officer, contributed much to what happened at sea during those 14 fateful days. Awarded Vir Chakra

Late Captain S. PRAKASH
Commanding Officer INS Vikrant. Suraj the Navigator. Later Vice Chief and Director General Coast Guard.

A quiet, cool, painstaking specialist navigating officer with command experience of INS Khukri. Learnt his onions as Nanda's navigator. One can picture him with a toothpick, sitting in his Captain's chair of Vikrant as Flag Captain, and dealing the cards of war in the East, which was spearheaded by the carrier. Awarded Maha Vir Chakra.

Captain M.P. AWATI
Commanding Officer INS Kamorta (P 31). Manohar to friends. Later Vice Admiral—Flag Officer Commanding-in-Chief West.

A bearded, imposing quintessential 'old seadog'. He held sway with his abounding vocabulary, booming voice and military gait. With command experience of INS Betwa, this communication specialist came to grips with handling the lively Petya squadron he commanded with distinction in the Bay in 1971. Awarded Vir Chakra.

Late Captain M.N. MULLA
Commanding Officer INS Khukri and F 14. Masterji to friends.

A brilliant Naval officer from a family of lawyers. Targeted by a Pak submarine torpedo attack, he went down with his ship, smoking his last cigarette in the old traditions of the Navy, made famous by Melville de

 Mello on radio. A loved Captain for his Urdu, replete with slang. The way he dealt cards at bridge will long be remembered with nostalgia. Awarded Maha Vir Chakra posthumously.

Late Cdr B.B. YADAV
Badru to friends. Later Cmde.

This lucky Commander of the 25th Missile Boat Squadron took his well worked up boats to Karachi. He went on to win a Maha Vir Chakra for his support in this now famous attack on Karachi. The other missile killers The reader will encounter are Jerry Jerath, I.J. Sharma, Kavina and Omi Mehta who all went to Karachi with courage and scored hits. All awarded Vir Chakra

Late Captain M.K. ROY
Later Flag Officer Commanding-in-Chief East. Mickey to friends. Director Naval Intelligence in 1971.

This Royal Navy-trained Naval Observer commissioned the Cobra Alize Squadron 310 in 1961 in the UK. With his Bengali background and astute brain, he made a valuable contribution to improve the Navy's Intelligence set-up in 1971 and in providing assistance to the Mukti Bahini. Awarded PVSM.

Lieutenant Commander S.K. GUPTA
Later Commanding Officer, INS Vikrant —1984. Giji to friends.

This quiet unassuming boxer and ace pilot, with a blue from the NDA commanded the gallant 300 Seahawk Squadron of Vikrant. Under his leadership the Hawks flew a total of 123 sorties in 14 days with devastating effect on Cox's Bazar, Chittagong and Chulna. Awarded Maha Vir Chakra. Later Rear Admiral

Late Lieutenant General J.S. AURORA
General Officer Commanding-in-Chief Eastern Command. Later Member of Parliament.

A tough and unassuming Sardar who led the Eastern Army on a 14-day trail-blazing march into East Pakistan and used airborne support to cross rivers and bypass main towns. With his brilliant Chief of Staff Lt. Gen. J.F.R. Jacob, he devised the tactical moves to go to Dacca and supported the Mukti Bahini. Both kept their fingers crossed that China would not intervene. Awarded Padma Bhushan.

Late Air Marshal H.C. DEWAN
Air Officer Commanding-in-Chief, Eastern Command.
Harry to friends.

A quiet but forward-looking Air Marshal who overcame the paucity of air power at his disposal, and made the best use of sister Services and the

Navy's air arm but at times took the credit for Naval actions. Awarded Padma Bhushan.

LATE RICHARD NIXON
President, USA. Tricky Dick and Foxy Nixon to friends and opponents.

Nixon was in the thick of Watergate when the Indo-Pak war erupted. Pro-Pakistan to the core. Disclosures of US Navy movements by Yeoman Ratford in the National Security Council upset him. He had unpleasant words for Mrs. Gandhi. Claimed credit for the ultimate cease-fire (questioned in this book). Has later said that nuclear weapons may have been resorted to, if things had got out of hand.

HENRY KISSINGER
Nixon's Secretary of State. Henry to friends.

The Professor postured as the "know-it-all" for the world. This globe-trotting Secretary of State was advance man for Nixon and vacillated over feelings for India. Keen to open dialogue with China, he was bullied by Yahya Khan to choose between Mujib and himself. He is widely quoted to have said, "I am getting hell every half hour from the President (Nixon) that we are not being tough enough on India."

Late ZULFIKAR ALI BHUTTO
Prime Minister of Pakistan. Zulfi the Sindhi to friends.

He signed the Simla Agreement. Played a double game with Yahya and Mujib. An Oxford educated leader of Pakistan whose Pakistan People's Party (PPP) won only 60 per cent of the votes in West Pakistan 1970 elections, and should have bowed to Mujibur Rahman who claimed 291 out of 343 seats to form the central government. This was not palatable to Bhutto and the oligarchy in West Pakistan. He sided covertly with the military. After the war he met Mujib in Bhawalpur jail to try to work out a deal. He was done in by General Zia-ul-Haq.

Late Colonel M.A.G. OSMANY
Commander-in-Chief, Mukti Bahini.

A lesser man would have given up. A brilliant officer of the East Bengal Regiment who never married and was known as the "Father of the Regiment". Retired after a brush with Field Marshal Ayub Khan in the 1960s, but became head of Mukti Bahini. He was later Commander-in-Chief Bangladesh and then joined politics.

Late Admiral of the Fleet SERGEI GORSHKOV
(This author thrice served as his Liaison Officer in India)

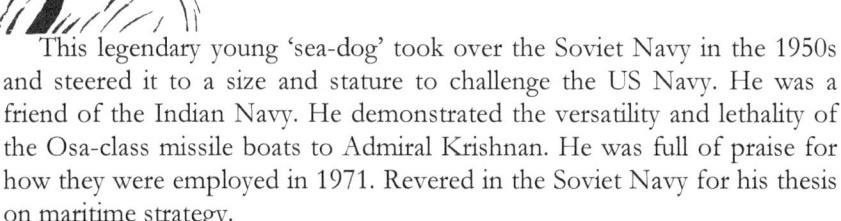

This legendary young 'sea-dog' took over the Soviet Navy in the 1950s and steered it to a size and stature to challenge the US Navy. He was a friend of the Indian Navy. He demonstrated the versatility and lethality of the Osa-class missile boats to Admiral Krishnan. He was full of praise for how they were employed in 1971. Revered in the Soviet Navy for his thesis on maritime strategy.

THE INDIAN NAVY SAILOR
In his first big test, he did admirable duty for the finest Navy.

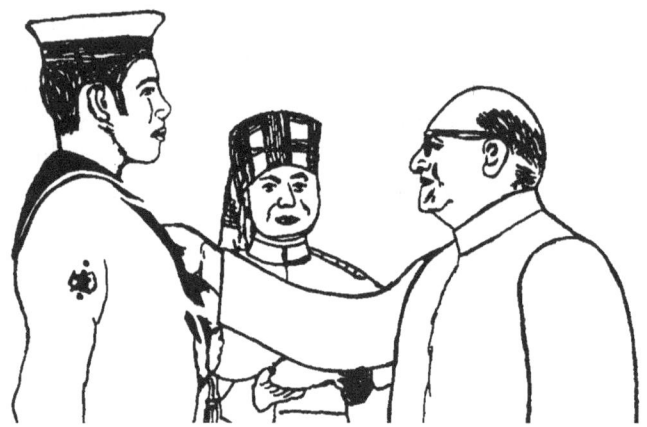

Representative of the unnamed thousands of officers and sailors who went into action on their ships, manned the hardware, did their duty with courage, and gave their all for the glory of their Service.

IN EACH SHIP THERE IS ONE MAN WHO IN THE HOUR OF EMERGENCY OR PERIL AT SEA CAN TURN TO NO OTHER MAN. THERE IS ONE WHO ALONE IS ULTIMATELY RESPONSIBLE FOR THE SAFE NAVIGATION, ENGINEERING PERFORMANCE. ACCURATE GUNFIRE AND MORALE OF HIS SHIP. HE IS THE COMMANDING OFFICER. HE IS THE SHIP.

BRONZE PLAQUE OFFICEOF CHIEF OF NAVAL OPERATIONS

U.S.A.

THE ORDER OF BATTLE – INDIA AND PAKISTAN

Modern warfare is an intricate business about which no one knows everything and few know very much.
—*Frank Knox*

The year 1971 marked 24 years of existence of India and Pakistan as separate entities. Pakistan had been under a military regime ruled by Gen. Ayub Khan since 26 March 1969, and the Pakistani Army had become a somewhat mercenary force. The Army had experienced successes against its own population in East Bengal and also in West Pakistan to fulfil the dictates of its masters. This had given the Navy a back seat position and Pakistan Navy's cooperation with Pakistan Air Force was poor, as is indicated in a Pakistani author's words in the chapter on "Causes of Pakistan's Defeat". Yet the silent service of Pakistan had built up an able submarine arm with three modern and one oldish boat from USA. The Pakistan Navy had a credible surface force of seven old British warships who together with their under-sea force were required to face a Navy with very recently inducted missile forces of the Osa class, and a somewhat more modern lot of ships and a proud Naval air arm with an old aircraft carrier, INS Vikrant in its arsenal. The odds were in favour of the Indian Navy, which fact was even accepted by Yahya Khan, but the Pakistan Navy tacticians were hopeful of their submarines playing a sneaky role which is what submarines are designed for. However, few fleets can operate without air cover in today's warfare at sea, and both navies lacked this feature in the West, since the Vikrant got assigned to the East.

The Pakistani View—Defence Plans

Pakistan has always had a good level of staff work and the British officers who stayed with that country longer, instilled into their thinking the axiom that "Planning for war is a continuous process. The higher defence organization of the country, consisting of military and political institutions should ensure that the war aim set is attainable". Regrettably, in 1971, Pakistan lacked a satisfactory higher defence organization, and the war aim, due to the East Bengal civil war was not defined. Hence the country suffered from the lack of both. This is discussed in the chapter "Causes of Pakistan's Defeat."

It appears that in 1970, the Military Operations Directorate defined the mission of the Armed Forces as one to defend the territorial integrity of Pakistan and in the process to destroy to the maximum the enemy's invading forces and to capture as much of the enemy's territory as possible by counter offensive. In August 1970, in a war game lasting four days it was proved that the offensive could only be met in the West. Later an exercise Titu Mir in the winter of 1970 also lent many lessons. The Army was reorganized with two independent armoured brigades and by August 1971, the plans were updated to counter-attack in the East and West. The defence of Dacca in the East was given importance and BOP (Border Outpost) posture adopted in the East. The Pakistani appreciation conceded Indian Air and Naval superiority in the East. It also assumed six Indian Division would be deployed in the East.

In the West. Gen Hamid Khan had planned to allow India to occupy the untenable Bambanwala-Ravi-Bedian (BRB) so as to enable a counter-offensive by his I Strike Corps to secure Jammu Tawi and Poonch: IV Corps moved from Lahore and 18 Infantry Division was to look after the 500-mile-long Rajasthan Kutch Sector (see Map).

Maritime Strategy

Maritime strategy is the total response of a nation to the oceans around it, for which sea power is required to achieve economic, political and military goals at sea. The Indian Navy boasted of a 1944-vintage aircraft carrier, the Vikrant (formerly HMS Hercules), one cruiser INS Mysore (formerly HMS Gambia), INS Delhi (formerly HMS Achilles, in docks), six frigates, eight missile boats and four submarines in the main. The overall strategy of India was, as hitherto, to use the Army and Air Force for the main thrust and to project itself through the Navy in the Indian Ocean and attempt to hold superiority over the Pakistanis. India could also boast of an indigenization programme of building warships and INS Nilgiri (F 33, 2,080 tonns), the first Indian Leander with modern fire-control equipment, Sea Cat surface-to-air missiles and an Alouette helicopter was getting ready after her preliminary sea trials. India had already turned out a survey ship, INS Durshak, and a number of seaward defence boats. But it was inadequately equipped for maritime reconnaissance, and important element of war.

The merchant-ship building industry in India was well developed by 1971 and it would be correct to assume that with India's position as the tenth largest navy in the world, and also near-ninth position in the mercantile marine, India did have a defined maritime strategy. It was up to Indian naval tacticians to use their forces judiciously from India's three major Naval bases and a number of ports from where offensive action could be launched.

Pakistan on the other hand had a minimal sea-going navy was superior in the quality of submarines, had a shipbuilding facility in inception, but an adequate ship repair yard. It had only one major naval base in the West, Karachi, and its deterrence to India for which it had planned assiduously, even as it does today. It had a proud and efficient submarine arm to keep the Indian Navy guessing, adequate maritime reconnaissance aircraft to scour the seas and vintage surface warships for hold-back operations at sea. It could not expect to seek battle with the Indian Navy whose gun power and missilery was superior but it hoped to safeguard its coastline and deliver deadly probes with its submarine arm. Hence their maritime strategy was one of infancy based on deterrence.

Manpower and Equipment

The ethnic origins of Indian and Pakistani seamen are the same and if dressed in the same uniform would be indistinguishable. The Indian Navy had a similar work force as the Pakistani Navy comprising a strength of 25,000 with an edge of 10,000 in personnel. The technical arms of both the navies were manned by adequately trained personnel though the advantage lay with India, as a number of technical sailors in the Pakistani Navy were from East Bengal. The East Pakistanis had been taken off sensitive posts and some had even fled. The international Press had also reported that some Bengali sailors had deserted their latest Daphne Pakistan Navy submarine Mangro at Toulon on a homeward passage after commissioning and work-up.

The Indian Navy had only some months earlier acquired eight missile boats of the Osa class and the crews were freshly trained in the Soviet Union. The naval pilots of the Indian Navy were a class of superior-grade fliers and those who were away from flying duties were called back to the carrier, and flew as a team irrespective of rank or seniority. This made the Vikrant a formidable machine even though she was aging. The Seahawks and Alizes on board were airworthy and able. The Indian Navy had also recently commissioned a squadron of Seakings from Westland Aviation, UK but the crew had no tactical training since the weapon fits were still being inducted. At best therefore, they were good and efficient flying machines, yet to be worked up and integrated with the Western Fleet. The Seakings were flown to Bombay post-haste just when the war broke out. The Indian Naval Fleets, both Eastern and Western, were manned by an excellent band of professionals with some of the Indian Navy's finest officer material in command. Most Captains had exposure to fine Royal Navy training and all-round experience.

Thus, overall the Indian Navy was in good shape. Their Chief, Admiral S.M. Nanda, was brilliant tactician with a charisma all his own, combined with that very special quality that leadership demands. He was one of the more forward-thinking Service Chiefs the Ministry of Defence has seen. His background as an official in the Karachi Port Trust before joining the Navy gave him knowledge of the port of Karachi. The later commands of INS Mysore (flagship), the Western Fleet, Western Naval Command and the meetings he had with that wise old man, Admiral Sergei Gorshkov had given him the deep insight of how to judiciously use his arsenal comprising Eastern and Western origin ships.

In comparison, the Pakistani officers were relatively younger, had seen quick promotions and not had the benefit of intensive work-ups for lack of fleet support and poor Pakistan Air Force cooperation. This has been admitted by many Pakistani authors including Gen. Fazel Muqueen Khan. Their Chief, Admiral Hasan was aware of all these lacunae which possibly gave him the clear line of tactics; to be aggressive with his submarine arm, and defensive on all other fronts till the Indian Naval Fleet was located. Such was the line-up of the two Navies in 1971. The order of battle with the Indian Command list is given as per the 1971 Janes Fighting Ships. This sets the scene of what did follow. In the East, Rear Admiral Sharrif had a small band of officers, gunboats and patrol craft and it was left to him to use his ingenuity to employ whatever tactics he could. His objective was to use his forces when not engaged in helping the Army to control the populace, and to patrol the coast. He never anticipated the havoc the aircraft carrier would create and trusted the Ghazi to stalk the Indian Eastern Fleet which included the Vikrant. In the West Rear Admiral Lodhi (Compak) was left with no choice but to send his submarines a field and keep his ships closer home.

Naval Orbat - India -1971

President – Mr. V.V. Giri
Prime Minister – Mrs. Indira Gandhi
Defence Minister – Mr. Jagjivan Ram
Finance Minister – Mr. Y.B Chavan

Administrative
Defence Secretary – Mr. K.B Lall
Home Secretary – Mr. Govind Narain

Naval Command
Chief of Naval Staff- Admiral S.M Nanda, PVSM
Vice Chief of Naval Staff - Vice Admiral J. Cursetji, PVSM
Flag Officer C-IN-C Western Naval Command - Vice Admiral S.N Kohli, PVSM
Flag Officer C-IN-C Eastern Naval Command - Vice Admiral N Krishnan, PVSM, DSC
Flag Officer Southern Naval Area - Rear Admiral V.A. Kamath, PVSM

Naval Fleet
Aircraft Carrier(1) Diesel Submarine(4) Cruiser(2) Destroyer(3) Escort Destroyer(3) Frigate(19) Survey ship(3 ex frigates) Ocean Minesweeper(1) Coastal Minesweeper(4) Inshore Minesweeper(4) Torpedo Boat(6) Seward Patrol Craft(15) Support Ship & Service Craft(16)

Naval personnel
20,000 Personnel (1800 Officers, 18,200 Ratings)

Naval Bases and Establishments
Bombay (C-IN-C Western Fleet, Barracks and Main Dockyard); Visakhapatnam (C-IN-C Eastern Command and fleet, Submarine Base, Dockyard and Barracks; Cochin (Naval Air Station, barracks and Professional Schools); Lonavala & Jamnagar (professional Schools); Calcutta, Goa & Port Blair (Small Bases)

Merchant Fleet
399 Vessels of 2.5 Million Tons Gross (LLOYDS Register of Shipping)

Indian Navy Western Feet - 1971
Rear Admiral EC Kuruvilla PVSM (FOCWEF
Fleet Ops Officer Cdr GM Hiranandani NM

INS Mysore flagship West (Capt RKS Ghandhi VrC)

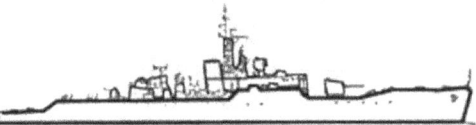

INS Trishul (Capt KMV Nair VrC) F-16
INS Talwar (Cdr SS Kumar VrC)

INS Kiltan (Cdr Gopal Rao MVC VSM), INS Kadmatt (Cdr S Jain NM)
INS Katchall (Cdr KN Zadu VrC)

INS Khukri (Capt MN Mulla MVC), INS Kirpan (Cdr RR Sood VrC NM),
INS Kuthar (Cdr VC Tripathi NM)

INS Ranjit (Cdr RN Singh)

A Nation and its Navy at War

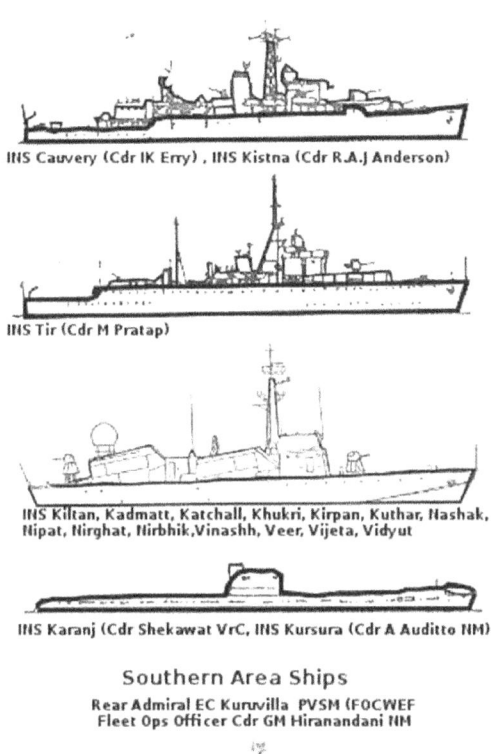

INS Cauvery (Cdr IK Erry) , INS Kistna (Cdr R.A.J Anderson)

INS Tir (Cdr M Pratap)

INS Kiltan, Kadmatt, Katchall, Khukri, Kirpan, Kuthar, Nashak, Nipat, Nirghat, Nirbhik, Vinashh, Veer, Vijeta, Vidyut

INS Karanj (Cdr Shekawat VrC, INS Kursura (Cdr A Auditto NM)

Southern Area Ships
Rear Admiral EC Kuruvilla PVSM (FOCWEF
Fleet Ops Officer Cdr GM Hiranandani NM

INS Amba (Capt VA Dhareshwar

INS Godavari (Cdr HD Singh), INS Ganga (Lt Cdr S Kulshetra

Eastern Fleet - 1971
Rear Admiral SH Sharma PVSM (FOCEF)
Fleet Operations officer Capt. SM Vyas

INS Vikrant - Flagship East (Capt S Prakash MVC)

INS Brahmaputra (Capt JC Puri VrC VSM) F16
INS Beas (Cdr L Ramdas VrC VSM)

INS Rajput (Lt Cdr Inder Singh)

INS Kamrota (Capt MP Awati VrC) P31
INS Kavaratti (S Paul VrC)

INS Khanderi (Cdr RJ Millan VrC)

Other Ships:

Landing Ship Tank - Magar, Ghariyal, Guldar
Patrol Craft - Panvel, Pulicat, Panaji, Akshay
Requisitioned Craft - Padma, Palash

Naval Orbat - Pakistan - 1971

President - Agha Yahya Khan
PSO - Lt General S.G.M.M. Peerzada
Chief of Staff - Gen. Abdul Hamid Khan
Chief of National Security – Major General Ghulam Umar
Foreign Minister - Z.A. Bhutto
Defence Secretary - Ghiasuddin Ahmed.
Chief of General Staff - Gen G.L.. Hassan
Chief Secretary (East) - Muzzaffar Hussein
Inspector General of Police – MA Chaudhary

Naval Command

C-IN-C and CNS – Vice Adm Muzaffar Hasan, HQA, SK
Chief of staff – Rear Adm Rashid Ahmad, SK, TQA
FOC PN East – Rear Adm Muhammad Sharif, SK

Naval Fleet

Cruiser(1) Destroyer(5) Frigate(3) Submarine(4) Tanker(1) Minesweeper(8) Gun Boat(2) Salvage Tug(1)

Naval Personnel

9900 (900 Officers, 9000 Ratings)

Merchant fleet

179 Vessels of 566022 Tons Gross (Lloyds Register)

Naval Ships

Western Fleet:
Cruiser - PNS Babur
Destroyers - Badr, Khaibar, Shah Jahan, Alamgir & Jahangir
Frigates - Tipu Sultan, Tughril, Zulfiquar
Daphné class Submarines - Mangro, Hangor and Shushuk.
Gun Boats: Sadaqat, Rafaqat
Midget submarines - Chariots
Minesweepers - Muhafiz, Mujahid, Moshal, Momin, Mukhtar, Mubarak, Mahmood & Munsif
Tanker - Dacca
Salvage Tug - Madadgar
Eastern Fleet:
Gunboats - Jessore, Rajshahi, Comilla & Sylhet
1 Tench class Submarine - PNS Ghazi

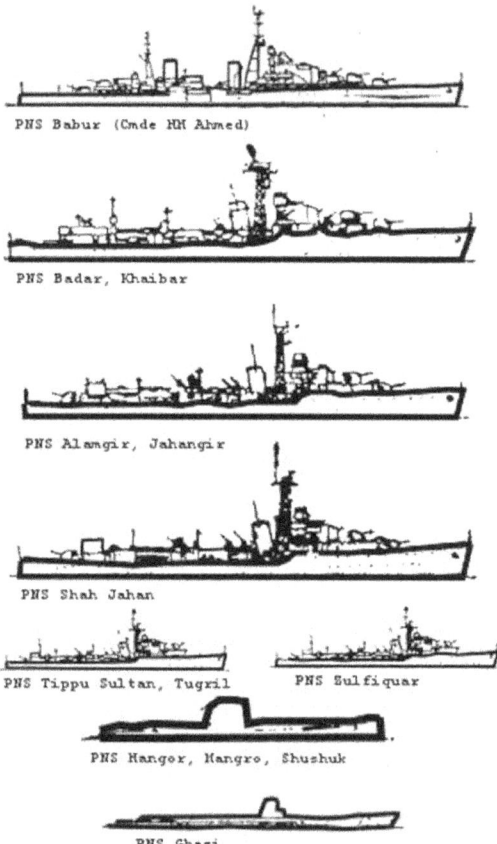

THE MUKTI BAHINI'S CIVIL WAR

The gates of our memories of Mukti Bahini will never close.
  How much we remember you, no one knows.
Deep in our hearts you will stay.
  You will always be remembered for that you last day,
So dear God, give them the message above
  Tell them we miss them
Offer them our love encore
  So that we can strive for them further more.

—In Memoriam

Ever since the reprisal of 25 March 1971 by the Pakistani Army, there was a slow and steady build-up of guerillas in East Pakistan and a Mukti Fauj (liberation army) had been formed with its units beginning to learn the art of guerrilla warfare. As Yahya Khan's soldiers spread death and destruction in East Bengal and raped women, saying cynically that they were providing better genes to the weak and Hindu-infected Bengali race, the hatred for the hoodlums in uniform increased. The activities of the Mukti Fauj, initially restricted to the country-side, engulfed East Pakistan in a civil war and the Army representing an ethnic minority attempted to quell the struggle. In the first few months they succeeded. Gradually, however, the armed opposition gained momentum, and as the monsoon advanced the Army found the guerillas becoming more audacious and ingenious in destroying bridges, ambushing Army units and resorting to unorthodox methods of warfare. Leaders like Abdul Haq and Mohammed Toaha objected to the mid-level Awami League cadre forming the Mukti Fauj and left it to the East Bengali Communist Party (EBCP) led by Maten Allaudin to lead a Maoist type of struggle. In Pabna, a military leader, Tipu Biswas, became a legend by his week-long attack on the Army unit there with success. By now, arms were being distributed and the population harboured the guerrillas. The guerrillas flushed out the Razakars and collaborators and weeded them out.

It is likely that contacts were made in India so that possibly havens were provided and training facilities were made available in India across the border. It is, however, plausible that the initial activities were left to the Mukti Bahini despite Pakistan allegations to the contrary.

Mukti Bahini

The guerrilla activities in East Pakistan by the Mukti Bahini (Liberation Army), having changed its name from the Mukti Fauj were greatly intensified from August 1971 onwards. The nucleus of the guerrilla forces now consisted of the East Bengal Regiment and the East Pakistani Rifles, which had rallied to the separatist cause. All sector commanders and many of their subordinates were former officers of the Pakistan Army. There was no dearth of volunteers in the wake of the outrages committed by the West Pakistani occupation forces who continued to indulge in murders, rape and subjugation of the East Bengalis. The Mukti Bahini force, as reported by the Guardian on 3 November 1971 rose to 80,000, almost equal to the 100,000 Pakistan soldiers stationed there. The exodus of refugees in India rose to nine million and many in India were willing to be trained and armed to go back for guerrilla operations. Pakistan Government statements constantly referred to the guerrillas as Indian agents or miscreants, but it is quite possible only training and safe havens were provided covertly by India and no more.

The politically sensitive elements in East Bengal had always encouraged political activity by students who had formed such groups as the Jangi Bahini (pro-Russian militant corps), pro-China Mukti Committee, Mukti Jot (NLF) and such organizations which were styled after Chairman Mao Zedong and Che Guevera. Hence motivational material was available for exploits against the Pakistan Army.

During the war an exclusively female Bichchu (Scorpion) party also came up. Suicide squads were a highlight of this party. On 11 April 1971 the formation of the Mukti Bahini was officially announced by Tajuddin Ahmed, Prime Minister of the recently proclaimed Bangladesh government operating from Calcutta, and on 14 April Col M.A.G. Osmany became the Commander-in-Chief. The command structure was provided by ex-Pakistan Army Bengali officers and the scene for organized activities against the occupation army was set.

The Mukti Bahini sank three ships in Chittagong harbour during the night of 15-16 August and an oil tanker on 3 November. Pakistan radio on 28 September claimed that the Pakistan Navy had killed 10 frogmen (clearance divers) who had been trained to lay limpet mines in Chittagong and Chalna harbours. Small river craft armed with 40/60 Bofors also made forays up the Chalna river and carried out sporadic shelling of ships going up to Chittagong and Chalna. There could be little doubt that some of this naval activity of the Mukti Bahini was supported by India by way of training and equipment though no actual personnel help was given.

On 12 September it was reported that 90 per cent of the culverts and small bridges between Dacca and Comilla, Jessore and Kustia were destroyed. The Mukti Bahini also directed their attacks against cargo ships and river craft.

On the political front on 8 September a consultative committee consisting of four Awami League representatives and four from other parties was formed in Calcutta to "direct the struggle for freedom". The

National Awami Party was represented by Maulana Abdul Hamid Bhashani and Professor Muzaffar Ahmed, the respective leaders of the pro-Chinese and pro-Soviet factions. There were defections by Pakistan diplomats the world over who gave support to the Provisional Government of Bangladesh. Abdul Fateh, Ambassador to Iraq gave up his post in August; Khurrum Khan Panni, Ambassador to the Philippines announced his resignation on 14 September, accusing the Pakistan Army of "history's greatest genocide". The list goes on: Mohinuddin Ahmed Jogiondar, Political Counsellor in Lagos; Rhezaul Karim, Political Counselor in London; Wali-Ur-Rahman, the deputy head of the Pak Embassy in Switzerland, Humayun Rasheed Chaudhry, Minister-Counsellor and Head of the Pakistan High Commission in New Delhi announced his defection on 4 October to head the unrecognized mission of Bangladesh. These developments created a communication link between the Indian Government and the Mukti Bahini, which was later to aid and assist the Indian armed forces, especially the Army in its thrust in December. Ex-Navy personnel/river guards helped navigate craft up tricky rivers.

On 11 November the Daily Telegraph reported that seven major regions had been declared as liberated zones by the Mukti Bahini. Pakistani troops are believed to have kept to their barracks by night. The Mukti Bahini attacks were directed towards disruption of communications, bridges and culverts.

Guerrilla groups operating inside Dacca were reported to consist largely of students. They bombed the International Hotel early in September and became increasingly active in October, when they made an unsuccessful attempt to shell the airport. Guerrillas disguised as Pakistani soldiers entered the city's main power station on 3 November and destroyed three of the four main generators, bringing industry to a stand-still within a 30-mil radius, whilst other guerrilla activities in Dacca during this period escalated to include the bombing of educational institutions, which were under the Army's control, and a series of armed bank robberies. A curfew was imposed on the city on 17 November while the Army carried out a house-to-house search for arms; Pakistan Radio subsequently reported that 138 people had been arrested and four killed while resisting arrest. Two West German diplomats had previously been killed 15 miles from Dacca on 14 November when their vehicle drove over a land mine.

The guerrillas also pursued a policy of assassinating persons collaborating with the Pakistan Government and the Army. Abdul Monem Khan a prominent Muslim League politician was shot dead at his home in Dacca on 14 October. The Governor of East Pakistan, Malik, who had been accused of being responsible for the shooting of civilians during popular demonstrations against President Ayub Khan's regime in 1968-69 was another victim. A candidate who had recently been returned unopposed to the Provincial Assembly was shot dead near Dacca on 7 November, and another in the Rajshahi district on 12 November.

Reprisals

Reports by refugees entering India alleged that the Army and the Razakars (the civilian militia) had let loose a virtual reign of terror as a reprisal for the guerrillas' activities. These allegations appeared to be confirmed by Western correspondents in East Pakistan.

The Times reported on 12 September: "Military terror is continuing in East Pakistan …. Political suspects are still 'lifted', although care is taken to make their arrests unobtrusive. Army reprisals continue to be savage. In the last week of August 17 suspects were taken from seven villages, line up and shot. Their homes were destroyed…."

A New York Times correspondent, Sydney H. Schanberg reported from the Indian border on 21 September:

The dozens of refugees interviewed by this correspondent today, all of who fled into India from East Pakistan in the past week, describe the killing of civilians, rape and other acts of repression by the soldiers….Nearly all the latest arrivals are Hindus, who said that the military regime was still making the Hindu minority kits particular target. They said the guerrillas were active in their areas, and that the Army carried out massive reprisals against civilians after every guerrilla raid…. According to the refugees, the Army leaves much of the 'dirty work' to its civilian collaborators—the Razakars, or Home Guards—it has armed, and to the supporters of rightwing religious political parties such as Moslem League and Jamaat-i-Islam.

A Reuters correspondent, Fred Bridgland, who watched about 400 refugees cross into India in about three hours, reported on 12 November that before they crossed the border they had told him similar stories. He wrote:

An elderly Hindu cultivator whose family was in the group said the Razakars and Pakistan Army were "taking away our women and looting and burning the villages". He said the attacks usually followed night operations by the Mukti Bahini. Refugees from other districts also spoke of villages being burnt, women abducted and young men killed..

The Date—21 November 1971

Clashes between the Indian armed forces and the Pakistani Army on the Bengal border were often reported, with loss of life, and later names of Group Captain Khondekar (Chief of Staff) and Brig M.A.G. Osmany (C-in-C) of the Mukti Bahini were openly spoken about. Yet, till the official history is written, the Mukti Bahini offensive narrated in Kesing's Contemporary Archives is culled and reported, to close this chapter.

The fighting on the East Pakistan border was greatly intensified after Nov 21, when the Mukti Bahini launched an offensive against Jessore, reportedly with Indian support. Whilst Pakistani official statements attributed the fighting in this and other sectors of East Pakistan to the Indian armed forces, assisted by "Indian agents", Indian sources maintained that only the Mukti Bahini were involved. Western correspondents in the areas agreed that the Indian Army was supporting the guerrillas, but stated that its share in the fighting was exaggerated in Pakistani statements.

Miss Clare Hollingworth, the Daily Telegraph correspondent in East Pakistan, reported on Nov 29 that there could be no doubt that Indian troops were involved, and that she had talked with a wounded Indian sergeant in the military hospital at Jessore. She stated on the following day, however, that "in general the scale of the military operations has been mounted at more than battalion level, with the majority attacks made by no more than 120 infantry men or one company". The Times correspondent in Calcutta wrote on December 2: "Only two Indian brigades—perhaps three including reserves—were used secretly to support the front line Mukti Bahini in the Jessore area. Artillery was used, but there was no air cover, and the infantry assaults were left to the guerrillas." A Pakistani military spokesman in Rawalpindi admitted on Nov 28, for the first time since the offensive began, that Bengali guerrillas were fighting against the Pakistan Army and that "people in East Pakistan are by and large, assisting the guerrillas".

Indian tanks crossed the border in the Jessore sector on Nov 21, although it was officially stated that they had withdrawn after a limited defensive action. An air engagement in which at least two Pakistani aircraft were shot down occurred in the same area on the following day.

Pakistan Radio alleged on Nov 21 that two Indian brigades supported by a tank regiment and accompanied by "Indian agents", had attacked north-west of Jessore. On Nov 22 the Associated Press of Pakistan stated that the Indians had stopped their onslaught after fierce fighting in which they had lost 18 tanks and 130 men killed, against only seven Pakistanis killed; it also alleged that Indian aircraft taking part in the action had strafed three villages killing 79 civilians. Lieut-General A.A.K. Nizai (the Pakistani Commander in East Pakistan) told journalists on the same day that Indian troops had penetrated eight miles in the Jessore sector.

An Indian Defence Ministry spokesman denied on Nov 22 that India had launched an offensive in the Jessore area; stated that Indian troops had strict instructions not to cross the border; and declared that Pakistan, after describing the Mukti Bahini as "Indian agents", had now started calling them "Indian Army infiltrators". On Nov 22 however Mrs. Gandhi said in a statement to both Houses of Parliament: "On Nov 21 Pakistani infantry supported by tanks and artillery launched an offensive on the Mukti Bahini who were holding liberated areas around Boyra, five miles from our Eastern border. The Pakistani armour under heavy artillery cover, advanced to our border, threatening our defensive positions. Their shells fell in our territory, wounding a number of our men. The local Indian military commander took appropriate action to repulse the Pakistani attack. In this action 13 Pakistani Chaffee tanks were destroyed."

Although Mrs. Gandhi did not say whether the Indian tanks had actually crossed the border, a Government spokesman said later the same day that they had done so in order to meet the oncoming Pakistani tanks, and after advancing "a very short distance" into East Pakistan, had returned within a few hours without suffering any losses. Whereas the Indian forces had previously been under orders not to cross in any circumstances, he stated, following the Pakistani tank offensive they now had the right to do so, if under attack. He added that this incident was the only one so far in which Indian troops had actually crossed the border.

A defence Ministry spokesman stated on November 22 that four Pakistani Sabre jets had intruded about three miles into Indian airspace in the same area earlier the same day: that three of them had been shot down by Indian Gnat fighters; and that the pilots of two machines, who had bailed out, had been taken prisoner. A spokesman of the Pakistan Government admitted on Nov 23 the loss of two aircraft but claimed that they had been attacked on "a routine mission well within Pakistani territory" and that two Indian fighters had also been destroyed. An Indian spokesman denied on the following day that any Indian aircraft had been lost.

The Mukti Bahini launched an attack on Nov 23 on Chaugacha, an important road junction about seven miles north-west of Jessore which fell on Nov 29 after fierce fighting. The hamlet of Burinda (seven miles west of Jessore) was overrun by Indian troops on the following day. It was reported on Nov 30 that Colonel A.G. Osmani, Commander of the Mukti Bahini, had set up his headquarters near Jessore, and that leaders of the Bangladesh movement had moved into the area from Calcutta, in readiness to set up a Government in Jessore when it fell. The town was held over 3,000 troops however, operating from a well-prepared system of underground tunnels and concrete bunkers.

Against all these killings it was only Mukti Bahini which acted, it was only those unsung heroes who fought back against the Pakistani Army. They will soon be forgotten but this chapter is a dedication to the Mukti Bahini. The exact Indian connection will be available when official history is written but none can deny that India's case from August 1971 to assist the Mukti Bahini was laudable in the cause of human concern.

AMERICA'S ANTI-INDIA TILT

True friendship is a plant of slow growth and must undergo and withstand the shocks of adversity before it is entitled to the appellation.
—Washington 1783

One aspect of the Indo-Pak war which will always be debated is USA's partiality towards Pakistan—commonly termed as the 'tilt'. No discussion on what led to the war will be complete without considering the various aspects of the 'tilt'. President Nixon admits in his memoirs that in the midst of the Watergate scandal, the most explosive event of 1971 occurred at the end of the year half way around the world from America, on the Indian subcontinent. As the American President, his involvement was high and USA's role needs full expose in this book for he clouds the matter in his memoirs by taking credit for the cease-fire—Mrs. Gandhi, he is reported to have said, and with conviction, may have had designs on West Pakistan as well as on East Pakistan. The arrival of TG 74 (USS Enterprise Decatur Parsons) he claims, may have caused India to think twice because it was Nixon's personal order. In other words, the gesture may have been extremely timely and useful. More recently Nixon has indicated that the nuclear threat was also suggested through USSR. Of his meeting with Mrs Gandhi on 4 November 1971 he has written: "I later learned that even as we spoke Mrs. Gandhi knew that her generals and advisers were planning to intervene."

It is now amply clear to military and political observers that Mrs. Gandhi's decision to call for a cease-fire in the West soon after surrender in the East by General Niazi, was in no way dictated by TG 74's arrival in the Bay of Bengal or USA's nuclear threat if there was one. In fact, Naval Commanders were questioning the rules of engagement (battle rules) which would apply if an Indian Navy submarine came up with the American task force during the war. No clear-cut guidelines were issued except the earlier rules of positive enemy identification, which in fact hampered the actions of the Indian Navy submarines. Yet one could not, in the fog of war put it past a naval submarine captain to unleash a salvo of torpedoes, if ever he felt his own vulnerability and safety were being threatened, for that too is provided in the rules of engagement—to attack in self-defence. Whilst Nixon was convinced of his reasons for ordering the US task force into the Bay of Bengal as a deliberate step, Admiral Zumwalt, the then Chief of Naval Operations who incidentally was not consulted, was most unhappy. He claimed Nixon had sent the ships into 'harm's way', a term coined after Pearls Harbour. This, Zumwalt has elaborated in his book On Watch in a chapter entitled "The Tilt". Henry Kissinger was Secretary of State during this turbulent period and has devoted a full chapter to the "Tilt" and given his version of the 1971 war. In this context, it may be relevant to recall an incident in 1956 which is bound to have caused a deep personal pique to Kissinger and created in his mind a feeling of animus against Indians. N.K. Bhojwani has narrated this incident in the Indian Express of 28 March 1972 (Bombay edition) in an article entitled "The Tragedy of Henry Kissinger: From Image Maker to Image Breaker" Bhojwani was Secretary of the Department of Parliamentary Affairs in 1955 when he came to know Kissinger at the Harvard Seminar and was Principal of a college in Bombay when he wrote this article.

Henry Kissinger was the brain, heart and soul of an annual event which he organized for several years running at Harvard University. This was the International Seminar to which he invited intellectuals from several countries in Asia and Europe.... The seminar aimed at fostering understanding...and acquainting participants with the American way of life...Kissinger organized the seminar programme with great competence and imagination....He was keen to know the world through meeting men and women of learning and as a good American, project a good image of his country.... At the Harvard seminar in 1955 he suggested to me that I organize a seminar in India as a reunion of selected participants of previous seminars at Harvard.... He himself was of the view that India was a very important country in international affairs....and needed to be studied and understood. I agreed to his suggestion in principle....As the arrangements for seminar reached an advanced stage, it became known that Asia Foundation in US had a hand in financing the seminar. This Foundation was then suspect in India as a CIA channel...the organizing committee decided to abandon the project. It was my unpleasant task to inform Kissinger that for unforeseen reasons we felt compelled to cancel the reunion...the reason for this was not mentioned. Thus we missed an opportunity of educating Kissinger in Indian affairs on the spot and he missed an opportunity of making a leisurely study of India. He had every reason to resent this abrupt unexplained abandonment of a pet project of his. It is bound to have struck him as a clumsy recompense for the hospitality and cordiality extended to us by him and several other individuals and organizations in US.

This incident was of no significance in terms of political or international relations. But it is possible that it left a sense of personal resentment simmering in Kissinger's subconscious mind and was the root cause of his anti-India stance.

The American columnist Jack Anderson, Pulitzer Prize winner, who was to embarrass the US Administration by his exposures of its foreign policy often trained his guns on Kissinger. It is reported by Admiral Zumwalt that whilst Anderson was on a visit to India, the US Navy Yeoman (a yeoman is a senior sailor in the Signals and Communication Department) Chief Petty Officer Charles Ratford stationed in Delhi at the American Embassy was assigned as his Liaison Officer. An interesting friendship was struck between Anderson and Charles Ratford over meetings with many Indians. Anderson had grown fond of the people and the country. He therefore assiduously followed the events of 1971 and to his good luck this yeoman was then on the innermost secretarial staff of the National Security Council in Washington, with access to the highest secrets and discussions. It is claimed that Yeoman Charles Ratford, whose fondness and attitudes were pro-India was unhappy with the deliberations at the Council. It was he who leaked the deliberations of the Council to Anderson. This has been confirmed by Admiral Zumwalt in On Watch. He goes further to stress that when he tried to book this errant yeoman, he was prevented from taking any disciplinary action for fear of exposure. In fact all he was allowed to do was transfer Ratford to a Naval station furthest away from Washington. Zumwalt, the youngest CNO at 49, who superseded many admirals, was also to see his own downfall for not adhering to the US policies of Nixon and confronting his senior late Admiral Rickover (the legendary father of US nuclear submarines) on nuclear issues, though he successfully steered and reduced drug abuse and controlled black-white problems in the United States Navy.

The Tilt—As Kissinger Saw it

White House years shows that it had the trappings of an epic Greek drama, with a handful of characters, draped in robes of conflict, searching for a compromise in the hazy whirlpool of world politics. The world's largest democracies were at war ideologically and factually. Of special note in the book as regards the 1971 war, was America's pro-Pakistan tilt. The topic has no doubt been debated threadbare, but a first-hand account form three of the main characters, Kissinger, Zumwalt and Patrick Moynihan, has a unique questioning flavour. These are used as tools to endorse an opinion that the USA (after much procrastination) fuelled and abetted Pakistan. What began as measures of warm response turned into a warm handshake.

That the White House, with its two political denizens, Nixon and Kissinger, were "marooned in homeland" was common knowledge. The people of America seemed opposed to the Administration's posture of "tilt" (and when the foreign policy of a President is questioned by the majority of his own people, it gives reason for aliens to doubt the honorability of his intentions).

It was difficult, initially, to believe that the statements Kissinger makes in his book are his—so shorn are they of diplomacy and obliqueness. Take for instance:

The gulf in perception between the White House and the rest of the government became apparent in an option paper, prepared for the July 23, Senior Review Group Meeting. It recommended that, if China intervened in an India-Pakistan war, USA should extend military assistance to India, and should co-ordinate its resources with the Soviet Union and Great Britain... nothing more contrary to the President's foreign Policy, could ever be imagined, he repeatedly stated that we should lean towards Pakistan, but every prop that was made went contrary to his instructions.

The relevance of the issue, and India's stand on it were largely misinterpreted. India had been through the grinding misery of suppression. It identified with the misery of brutal killing—Indian hearts and minds were shocked beyond reason. They rose in unison to the aid of a humanitarian cause—to redeem their brethren from the shackles of repression, but that was not all. The disastrous effects on the economic and political structure of the country could not be ignored. The influx of refugees had swollen to alarming proportions. In such circumstances, to take the stand that it did, absolved India of the guilt of war but Kissinger had a contrary opinion. He insistently interpreted the Indian strategy "as a stand for preeminence on the subcontinent".

USA could have restrained Pakistan, enlighten it on the implications of war, and could have resorted to the ultimate weapon of withdrawing all support to the erring nation, but this did not happen. Kissinger justified it thus: "The victim of attack was an ally to which we had made many, explicit promises concerning precisely this contingency. Clear treaty commitments, reinforced by other undertakings dated back to 1959... we could not ignore them." At another place he states: "The fact was that over the decades of our relationship with Pakistan, there had grown a complex body of communications—some verbal, some in writing, whose plain import was that USA would come to Pakistan's assistance if attacked by India."

About Indo-US relations Kissinger writes: "By 1971 our relations with India had achieved a state of exasperatedly strained cordiality, like a couple that can neither separate nor get along...". The fact was that India was a nation of huge potential which USA needed to befriend, but "We (USA) moreover had every incentive to maintain Pakistan's goodwill. It was our crucial link to Peking and Pakistan was one of China's closest allies." He further elaborates: "The US could not condone a brutal military repression in which thousands of civilians were killed. There was no doubt about the strong arm tactics of the Pakistan's military, but Pakistan was our sole channel to Peking.... That USA was slowly, steadily and surely driving a wedge into its scanty relationship with India was apparent, but the final straw was the report that in spite of contrary assurance, a Pakistani freighter sailed from New York to Karachi with military equipment. The New York Times charged that Government with breach of faith and the Washington Post on 5 July could barely contain its outrage. It lashed out at "the astonishing and shameful record". "We have classic example", it wrote, "of how the system really works hidden from public scrutiny, administrative officials have been supplying arms to Pakistan, while plainly and persistently telling the public that such supplies were cut off". USA can never be exonerated for such duplicity.

A democratic nation, and its leaders, often claim a view that is free from partisanship of any kind. That in itself seems the essence of democracy, but mortals, rarely if ever, can transcend petty prejudices. Undoubtedly everyone is entitled to a personal opinion but if the opinion is to colour a decision of larger dimensions, it must stand the test of reason. Nixon, it is common knowledge, had a profound distrust of Indian motives, and this stemmed from his apparent dislike for the leader of the nation in question. To quote Kissinger, "Nixon had no time for Mrs. Gandhi's condescending manner. Privately he scoffed at her moral pretensions…and suspected that, in the pursuit of her purposes, she had fewer scruples than he." Nixon had labeled her "a cold blooded practitioner of power politics." Bhutto on the other hand was lauded for his doings, and was thought to be "elegant, eloquent, and subtle. Bhutto was at least a representative who would compete with Indian leaders for attention". Nixon later realized, but never admitted, that he had laid his bet upon a wrong horse.

The period 1971-86 is an eternity of 15 long years. Nixon is out of power and Mrs. Gandhi is no longer amidst us. Today when we stake tall claims to peace, equality and justice, this legacy of mutual distrust and harmony must end. It is time for India and Pakistan to bury their hatchets and channelise energies for more constructive and demanding purposes, and on evaluation, one issue stands projected straight and clear. If USA is to understand India, the so-called and apparent tilt must cease.

As Zumwalt Describes It

Some excerpts on the "tilt" from Zumwalt's book On Watch are necessary to the weaving of the Naval story as he throws light on the US Naval view.

The war provided a vivid illustration of the thesis I had presented to the President in August. The United States tilted towards Pakistan, but tilt as we would, we could not affect the war's outcome. We had no "relevant power" in that part of the world, even after we had sent Task Force 74, consisting of the nuclear carrier Enterprise and supporting ships, into the Indian Ocean as a token of our concern.

On the subject of Soviet entry and US response in the Indian Ocean he writes:

The pattern of Soviet expansion in the Indian Ocean was already clear when Henry Kissinger and I held our 6 November 1970 meeting, and we discussed its implications in some detail. On 9 November 1970 Kissinger promulgated National Security Study Memorandum 104, which called for "an assessment of possible Soviet naval threats to US interests in the Indian Ocean area and the development of friendly naval force and basing alternatives consistent with varying judgments about possible threats and interests over the 1971-1975 period.

These were the beginnings of Deigo Garcia.

On Pakistan specifically Zumwalt reveals: "A little later came NSSM 118 ordering a Contingency Study on Pakistan's secession. Finally NSSM 133 required contingency planning on South Asia. This piling of study upon study resulted in what I can only call a verbal mudslide."

The first response of the United States to these events was to stop military assistance to Pakistan—India had not received any since the India-Pakistan war of 1965—as one way, among others of inducing Pakistan to make concessions in East Bengal. However, the Pakistanis were stubborn and slow to respond and India was getting hotter fast.

Then, in July, Henry Kissinger astounded the world by showing up in Peking. That event was partly made possible, it is relevant to point out, by the good offices of Pakistan in helping review communication channels between the United States and China that two decades of disuse had all but atrophied. Indeed Pakistan was the starting point for the last leg of Henry's secret journey.

Alluding to the actual activity in the Pentagon and White House Zumwalt lists dates and meetings to show how unclear USA's intentions were:

The Washington Special Action Group met on India-Pakistan on 17 August, 8 September, 7 October, 22 and 23 November and 1, 3, 4, 6 and 8 December, a schedule that reflects accurately the administration's cycle of concern. As I reread descriptions of those events three and a half years later, I am struck most by the mood of bafflement they convey. All the principal members of WSAG were officials close to the top of the government, men presumably accustomed to and adept at influencing, if not shaping, events; Henry Kissinger in the chair, John Irwin or Alexis Johnson, both great professionals, from State, Dave Packard from Defense, Richard Helms or his deputy from CIA, Tom Moorer or occasionally one of us other chiefs from the Joint Chiefs, one of several top officials from AID. Yet the minutes show them—us—growing for and never finding a line of action that might make America a factor in the ever more turbulent situation on the subcontinent.

On Jack Anderson's revelations, Zumwalt notes:

A second notable feature of those minutes is their depiction of Henry Kissinger's increasing irritability, not to say fury, in the face of his persistent inability to divert India by as much as hair from the course it had chosen to pursue. Doubtless a statesman shouldn't take his failures, which are bound to occur, personally, but Henry is not the only statesman who does. It was with this aspect of the WSAG meetings that Jack Anderson, in his celebrated revelations of the WSAG minutes, had the most fun.

On the entry of the US Task Force into the Indian Ocean:

On 10 December, a Presidential order that was not discussed with the Navy in advance created Task Group 74, consisting of the nuclear carrier Enterprise and appropriate escorts and supply ships, and sent it steaming from the gulf of Tonkin, where the ships had been on station, to Singapore. The order did not specify what TG 74's mission war, nor could anyone, including the Chairman on the Joint Chiefs, tell me. In talking with Mel Laird and Tom Moorer I sought to be sure that these ships either had a mission or were not sent in harm's way.

Yet in harm's way they did go.

The superpower game in the Indian Ocean in the 1971 war is well summed up by Lieut. Commander W. Hickman, US Navy in the United States Naval Institute proceedings 1979:

Likewise, in the Indian Ocean the Soviet presence has raised the stakes in the game of naval diplomacy. During the Indo-Pakistan War of 1971, both the United States and the Soviet Union deployed significant naval forces to the Indian Ocean. At the outbreak of the war on 3 December, both superpowers had only a nominal naval presence. The Soviets moved first by deploying two surface-to-surface cruise missile (SSM)-equipped ships (a "Kynda-class" cruiser and a conventional submarine) from Vladivostok on 6-7 December to support the non-SSM-equipped ships already in the Indian Ocean. On 10 December, the United States formed Task Force 74, consisting of the attack carrier Enterprise CVAN-65), the amphibious assault ship Tripoli (LPH-10), three guided missile escorts, four destroyers, and a nuclear attack submarine, ordering them into the Andaman Sea shortly thereafter. In apparent response to the US Task Force, the Soviets deployed another task group consisting of a "Kresta" class cruiser, a "Kashin" class destroyer, and two submarines on 12-13 December. The deployments on both sides can be seen as an attempt to convince both allies and adversaries of the strength of the respective commitment to the area. Although the Soviet presence in all likelihood could not have prevented the US force from intervening militarily had that been its mission, it could have made such intervention very costly, both in military and political terms. The Soviet actions in this crisis are examples of how the Soviets can represent themselves as the adversaries of the "imperialist aggressors" and protectors of beleaguered nations. Thus can they reap huge propaganda benefits in the Third World.

The above is a US view but when viewed with Kissinger's and Zumwalt's description it is evident that the Indian Ocean has been looking for a local master. In 1971 the Indian Navy lifted its head as a potent tool for India's role in the Indian Ocean.

Interestingly, another view of the tilt is provided by Daniel Patrick Moynihan who explains the dilemma between the United Nation's legal stance and USA's personal interests.

The second large event of the Twenty Sixth General Assembly was the third Indo-Pakistan war. The quintessential conflict of the age: racial, religious, linguistic.

Herewith another duality. Nathaniel Glazier and I had organized a seminar at the American Academy of Arts and Sciences on the subject of ethnicity. We argued that the single largest theoretical failure of Marxism was its inability to predict or to account for the ever more salient role of ethnic conflict—racial, religious, linguistic—in the modern age. This was something the two of us had worked out together and it was not unoriginal. Yet more and more I was persuaded of the need to fight ethnic issues on ideological lines.

The Indo-Pakistan war offered an occasion. Pakistan, the autocracy, behaved with irredeemable brutality toward its own people in East Bengal. (Glazier, whose wife was Indian, supplied details and urged me to battle. When it comes to providing true motive force, perhaps ethnicity is all.) India, the democracy, had intervened. The United Nations sided with Pakistan, and legality, one supposed, was also on that side. But the United States was supporting Pakistan for far more complex reasons. They had done Kissinger the favour of getting him to china in 1971. For Nixon, there was the large concern of demonstrating to the Chinese—in the first test of a new relationship—that the United States was a reliable ally. Neither argument entirely persuaded me. I could only repeat to the President (who could listen, at least) that India was democracy. At the end of the General Assembly I appeared on 'Meet Press' and went over the argument in public. The President was wrong, I said, and the United States should be ashamed. The following summer, as I sat out the presidential campaign in a farm in upstate New York, it came to me that Nixon would now begin to see India as the one large, if not great, power he had not really dealt with in his first term, and that he would ask me to go there as Ambassador in his second. This he did, and I did—neither of us knowing he would not really have a second term.—*A Dangerous Place.*

How honest or guarded Kissinger has been in his memoirs has been questioned and it is public knowledge that whilst Kissinger now attempts to claim to have wanted peaceful settlement, he was all for appeasing Yahya Khan—Pakistan's drunken dictator. The Bangladesh problem should, in effect, have been the test for the US as she always boasted of being the propagator of peace, protector of the oppressed, the champion of liberty and custodian of fundamental rights. It is unfortunate that the United States' attitude to the Bangla problem was guided more by her friendship with Pakistan and gratitude to that nation's leaders for having opened up a US dialogue with China, rather than objectivity and adherence to proclaimed principles. It is also an indicator to the future trend. This tilt of 1971 could well have marked another turning point in India's quest to seek Soviet friendship and aid, especially on the arms front which the Soviets welcomed. If USA is to understand India, the tilt towards Pakistan has to cease.

THE PRE-WAR PERIOD
(SEPTEMBER-NOVEMBER 1971)

To climb steep hills requires slow pace at first.

—*Shakespeare, Henry VII*

From mid-October, air was tense and almost everyone in the defence forces in India and for that matter also those in 'civie' street knew that the massive influx of refugees with eight million of them already under India's care could not continue indefinitely without some kind of confrontation between India and Pakistan. War certainly loomed over the Horizon, but all diplomatic activity pointed to some agreement and high hopes were being pinned on Mrs. Gandhi's visit in November that year to the United States. Yet the situation on the eastern border was becoming increasingly unstable. The Mukti Bahini forces were stepping up their activity and some collusion of the fourth columnists between Indian armed forces, BSF and the Mukti Bahini guerrillas was going on. Many in Pakistan feared that in the event of war with India, the odds were overwhelmingly in India's favour. Even Yahya Khan had conceded that war with India would be military lunacy. Diplomatic observers in Delhi were uncertain of China's stance in the event of a war and it was also a moot point for Indian military planners to ponder over. Six-to-eight Indian divisions were poised on the East Pakistani border against three Pakistani divisions, and three Indian divisions faced China. The weather factor had ensured that no major action could take place during the south-west monsoon which lasts till September and so with snow falling in the foot-hills of the Himalayas in November, there would be some insurance against Chinese intervention. It is most likely that military planners advised Jagjivan Ram, the then Defence Minister and Mrs. Gandhi, that any action before end-November would prove counter-productive. The 51-year-old Awami League leader Sheikh Mujibur Rahman was also under house arrest in West Pakistan and awaiting trial by court martial for waging war against Pakistan. As the date for the trail shifted from 11 August when it began to 7 September, it is quite possible the Government of India agreed to be patient till November as it suited India.

The Press Notes issued by the Martial Law Administrator on 19 August and on 28 September 1971 on Sheikh Mujibur Rahman's trial are telling and Kevin Rafferty's report in the Financial Times, London, dated 12 October 1971 sums up the situation.

PRESS NOTE GIVING DETAILS OF TRIAL AND WARNING AGAINST CONTEMPT OF COURT

It will be recalled that a Special Military Court was convened by the Chief Martial Law Administrator to try Sheikh Mujibur Rahman in camera for waging war against Pakistan and for other charges.

The trial commenced on August 11, 1971. The court, however, adjourned the same day in order to ensure fair trial and justice so that Sheikh Mujibur Rahman could have a defence counsel of his own choice.

On September 7, 1971 the services of Mr. A.K. Brohi and his three assistants, namely, Mr Ghulam Ali Memon, Mr. Akber Mirza and Mr. Ghulam Hussain were procured, and the examination of the prosecution witnesses started.

The prosecution has so far examined 20 witnesses in support of the charges preferred against Sheikh Mujibur Rahman. The trial is in progress with Mr. A.K. Brohi as the defence counsel.

The public will be informed of the further progress of the case in due course of time.

Meanwhile people should in their own interest refrain from saying or doing anything which may constitute a contempt of court or a breach of secrecy of the trial proceedings, or which may tend to prejudice the case of either the defence or the prosecution.

—The Dawn, Karachi 29 September 1971.

"MORE PEOPLE THAN IN LONDON"

The fact is however that the refugees are still piling into India at the rate of 40,000 a day; they now total more than 9 million. These are Indian figures but no independent observer has yet disputed them. India is managing to care for them at a cost of Rs 2.77 each a day. This is only 15p each a day but it adds up to almost £500 million a year for 9 million people. So far the rest of the world has promised Rs 1,150m (£62m), but has handed over only Rs 189m (£10.5m) of this.

To get the refugee figures into perspective; there are more refugees from Pakistan than there are people in London. They are as many as the inhabitants of the 25 largest English country boroughs put together. So many prosperous people in a confined space as the Indian border area would be a problem but these people are not prosperous; they are homeless. Mostly profession-less, jobless...

—Kevin Rafferty

Operations in the Eastern theatre were closely guarded. The personnel involved were tight-lipped. Army moves towards the East, induction of Bengali Naval officers and sailors into Calcutta under Cdr. M.N. Samant for covert operations. And news of Naval divers cohorting with Mukti Bahini forces did appear sporadically in the Press, but detail were never divulged. Lt. Cdr. Ashok Roy, popularly known as Aku (son of Maj Gen A.N. Roy), an ace Alize pilot was suddenly transferred from INS Rana where he was the TAS Officer, to Calcutta. When he appeared in Bombay in November after some operational duty off Bangladesh, he had lost weight, looked troubled and refused to answer questions. He was keen to take a week's leave and it appeared he had been witness to some loss of lives. An intelligent, gregarious and yet philosophical officer, he appeared anxious. With Vikrant his second home out at sea, he a pilot, kept wondering why he was not on the big flat top. By now Captain M.K. Roy was setting in the saddle of Naval Intelligence and was deciding what to do with such Bengali officers. The Bengali Captain who had commissioned the Cobra Alize Squadron in France in 1960 and embarked Vikrant, had revamped the Directorate of Intelligence with officers of caliber. He was geared-up and backed by the Ministry of Defence to execute under-cover operations to aid the Mukti Bahini. His knowledge of Bengali and the spoken language must have come in handy. The men on the scene of action at Calcutta were Capt. R.P. Khanna, the Naval Officer Incharge and the specially selected Cdr M.N. Samant, a specialist navigator and a submarine Captain whose actions, as being nearest to East Pakistan, will remain secret till official history is written. He was awarded MVC.

Lt Cdr Jayanto Kumar Roy Chowdhry, a specialist gunnery officer was suddenly called away to Calcutta from the Gunnery School at Cochin. He was an East Bengali, uprooted after the partition and he had left behind his father who owned acres of land. Roy Chou, as he was popularly known, was upto tricks for East Bengal. A Shrapnel would in his leg in the war and the fact that his wife did not see much of him during pre-war months, could be indicators of the arduous duties he was engaged in. He was to lose his commandeered patrol craft the Padma to an attack from the Indian Air Force and earn himself a Vir Chakra. The story of this fine gallant officer's action is described in the war section of that day and in a separate chapter. Tempers run high in war. Disagreement between him and his boss—Cdr M.N. Samant, MVC, may have led to his career in the Navy being cut short, as has happened to many other decorated soldiers, sailors and airmen.

A number of naval divers from Command Clearance Diving Teams were transferred to Calcutta. Lt Cdr Sajjan Kumar, a pious and God-gearing clearance diver must have served many a daring mission along with his UK-trained colleagues, Lt Cdr G.C. Martis, B.C. Mahapatra, MCPO-II and Leading C. Singh, MVC. Not much is known of their activities but they were decorated for heroic action—there will be a number of others whose praises can only be sung when the official records are released. In this book I have published the official diary released by the Government of India which does not specifically indicate any naval activity prior to the war. It was possibly limited to training and provision of havens.

October 15	Pakistani troops, supported by heavy equipment, had been massed along the international border. Indian villages in Hilli and Radhikpur areas of West Dinajpur were intermittently shelled by Pakistani troops.
October 16	Mines planted by Pakistani saboteurs recovered near Agartala and between Barigram and Kaniai Bazar stations of the North-Eastern Frontier Railway. One Sub-Inspector was killed and two Border Security Force men injured as a result of the explosion of the mines, 8 miles south-west of Agartala.
October 17	Pakistani troops opened unprovoked firing on Indian territory near Shikarpur in Nadia district. Pakistani armed personnel intruded into Indian territory at Barman-Para border village near Mahendra Ganje in Garo Hill District of Meghalaya and opened fire.
October 18	Pakistani troops opened artillery fire across the international border in Belonia area, 42 miles south-east of Agartala.
October 19	Pakistani Army fired on Belonia town.
October 20	Four persons were killed when Kamalpur was heavily shelled by the Pakistani Army. A higher secondary school building and telephone line in the town were damaged.
October 21	Pakistani troops started unprovoked shelling on the Indian border village of Hilli. The Border Security Force returned the fire.

Two bogies attached to a goods train running between Karimganj and Dhrmanagar were derailed as a result of the explosion of a mine, two miles south of Karimganj. On the same day, a culvert and a wooden bridge were damaged by Pakistani saboteurs south-east of Belonia.

October 23 Pakistani saboteurs destroyed a bridge near Mohanpur on the Agartala-Simla road, which is a vital link with the northern part of the state. Pakistani troops also shelled Kamalpur town and Hilli area.

October 24 Five persons including one child were killed and 25 injured in an unprovoked heavy Pakistani shelling on Agartala and Kamalpur and some villages in Karimganj.

Two Sabre-jets of the Pakistan Air Force violated Indian air-space over Agartala.

October 25 Pakistani troops fired several rounds of light machine gun at Talai Bazar on the Karimganj border.

October 26 One person was killed and six injured when the Pakistan Army shelled the Indian border village of Hakimpur.

October 27 The Pakistan Army shelled Dharmanagar town and also continued shelling of Kamalpur town. Pakistani troops also fired with MMG across the border at Belonia. On the night between October 27 and 28, a company plus of Pakistani troops attacked a Border Security Force post near Jalpaiguri. The civilian airport was hit by bullets fired across the border.

October 28 This was the seventh day of heavy shelling of Kamalpur town. Pakistani troops also fired indiscriminately on Fakirpara and Toundipara.

October 29 Pakistani troops continued heavy shelling of Kamalpur town. It caused heavy damage to village adjacent to Kamalpur. One hundred Razakars raided the border village of Dalgaon and looted several houses.

Four refugees were burnt to death and three badly injured as a result of firing by Pakistani saboteurs in a refugee camp near Shillong.

Activities of Pakistani saboteurs in Tripura, Meghalaya and Cachar caused damage to bridges. At one place, the Border Security Force recovered six kilograms of explosives in Srinagar, near Agartala.

October 30 Provocative activities of the Pakistan Army were stepped up all along the borders. Indian troops tried to silence Pakistani guns by firing from inside Indian territory. It was explained by the government spokesman that Indian troops had "scrupulously avoided and 'hot chase' of the Pakistan Army into their territory." He added Indian action had so far been limited to warding off Pakistani attacks on their positions within Indian territory.

Shelling of Indian territory at scattered points in Tripura, Assam and West Bengal was reported.

November 1 Further Pakistani shelling of Kamalpur caused a number of civilian casualties and destroyed several buildings. The Border Security Force took preventive action to stop the shelling.

November 2 Pakistani troops kept up tension all along the Nadia border and resorted to unprovoked shelling of Indian borders.

November 3 An official spokesman said in a Press briefing that the Indian Border Forces which had silenced the Pakistani guns shelling Kamalpur did not cross the international border. "Indian artillery based in defensive emplacements within the Indian territory knocked out Pakistani guns. Our Army has strict orders not to cross the border."

November 8 An official spokesman reiterated that Pakistani guns had been silenced without Indian troops crossing the border.

November 12 Ten 60 mm mortar bombs were fired by Pakistani troops on Indian territory near Agartala. Shelling of other Indian area was also reported.

November 13 A massive thrust in battalion strength by Pakistan forces into Shikarpur village of Nadia district was mounted. Pakistani troops attempted to overrun the Indian border outpost. The Border Security Force assisted by Indian troops hurled back the Pakistani force after a heavy exchange of fire.

November 15 An official spokesman said that Indian troops did not pursue the attackers into East Bengal because they had orders not to cross the border.

November 16 Many reports of provocative acts by Pakistani troops in Tripura, Meghalaya, Assam and West Bengal were received. Seventy-five refugees had been killed or wounded when Pakistani artillery indiscriminately shelled the village of Bakshinagar in Tripura.

November 19 Intrusion of Pakistani troops into West Bengal and Meghalaya.

November 21 Eight Indian nationals were killed and 7 injured when Pakistani troops resorted to unprovoked shelling of Karimganj.

November 23	Four Pakistani Sabre-jets which intruded into Indian airspace on November 22 were shot down by Indian Air Force Gnats in an engagement north-east of Calcutta over the Boyra area.
November 23	Pakistan mounted a heavy attack with artillery and tanks on a liberated and 24 pocket in Boyra area. The Pakistani column advanced to the Indian border with all guns firing. Indian troops crossed and succeeded in throwing back the Pakistani attack destroying 13 Pakistani Chaffee tanks.
Nov 25 and 26	Indian troops crossed in self-defence into East Bengal to repulse a Pakistani column which was advancing with tanks towards Indian border posts in Hilli Area.
November 28	Indian troops which had crossed into East Bengal near Hilli returned to their post.
November 29	Indian Army had made a new defensive thrust in the Hilli area on November 27.
November 30	The battle in Hilli area where Indian forces had made a thrust to blunt incipient advances was continuing.
December 2	Pakistani Sabres strafed Agartala and shelled the town. Indian forces took appropriate action to safeguard Agartala.

The atrocities committed by the West Pakistani troops in East Pakistan were many and these came to better light after the war. Yet the war fever was evident in the Press reportage.

WAR FEVER IN PAKISTAN

With war fever mounting along the West Pakistan border with India, businessmen of Lahore are sending away their families or making plans to do so. Bank officials say many people are withdrawing their money or transferring their accounts to other cities. Peasant families are leaving their homes near the border. Motorists are decorating their cars with signs saying "Crush India".

Arnold Zeatling, Lahore A.P. Correspondent, 15 Oct 1971

INDIAN AND PAKISTANI ARMIES CONFRONT EACH OTHER ALONG BORDERS

The armies of India and Pakistan are now confronting each other along their borders.

Most Western diplomats here in New Delhi are inclined to believe that at least in West Pakistani troops moved up first and that the Indians moved in response.

According to high Indian sources, the build-up in West Pakistan began last month, and by last Thursday virtually all Infantry and Armoured Divisions in West Pakistan were at, or within, striking distance of the border.

Some border area canals have been flooded as barriers, and Pakistani civilians have evacuated several border areas, some on orders from the army and others on their own, out of panic, sources say.

Some of the heaviest troops concentrations are reported to be at points where the Pakistanis crossed the Indian border in the three-week war over Kashmir in 1965.

The border areas in East Pakistan, where it is believed there are four or five Divisions, have also reportedly been strengthened.

The Indians are also said to have four or five Divisions along their side of the border. President Agha Mohammed Yahya Khan of Pakistan has charged that the Indians have eight Divisions there.

At a heavily attended news conference this morning, Prime Minister Indira Gandhi was asked about urgings of the Great Powers for restraint.

"It seems very simple and plausible to say Pakistani troops will withdraw", she said. "But Pakistan has been escalating the situation by putting troops all along the border, by their hate-India campaign, and by their call for a war of Jihad (holy war). This is not a one-sided matter. You cannot shake hands with a clenched fist."

"As you know", she said, "everybody admires our restraint. We get verbal praise and the others who are not restrained—get arms support."

This was an apparent allusion to the continuation of some arms shipment to Pakistan by the United States.

—Sydney Schanberg, New York Times

The Indian armed forces were certainly worked up. The Navy assessed threats to shipping, opened a dialogue with ship-owners, beefed up intelligence, whilst the Fleets—the Western and the newly formed Eastern Fleet—spent more time at sea on manoeuvres than hitherto. The Western fleet saw itself foraying the Saurashtra coast calling at Okha whenever feasible, practicing navigation and dummy missile attacks in that region. The newly acquired missile boats under the command of USSR-trained officers and manned by a mix of Soviet-trained and locally Indian trained crews were put through their brisk paces. A missile-firing-on the battle practice target with direct hits gave confidence to men manning the boats and to the Senior Commanders and particularly the Chief of Naval Staff, Admiral S.M. Nanda, to plan special missile boat tactics in the event of war. These were also the fateful days when the Fleet practiced anti-submarine warfare, the biggest challenge that faces any fleet in the world. Lt V.K. Jain a bright electrical officer was permitted to research and experiment on INS Khukri's sonars, to enhance sonar detection, for surely the Indian Navy respected the strength in under-sea warfare of the Pak Navy through their newly acquired Daphnes and the PNS Ghazi (Defender of the Faith). It would be equally true that the Pak Navy were aware about the Indian Navy's fire and missile power and the range of the 'F' class ex-USSR submarines and depended a lot on their own submarines to foray forward, whilst their ships planned holding a defensive posture nearer home. Attention was paid to command and control aspects. Tactics were accordingly evolved. The arguments, professional in nature which crop up between a Fleet Commander (Chandy Kuruvilla) and his boss ashore (Kohli) is a common feature in all naval engagements before final plans are made. It was centered around the control of missile boats an got resolved. Interestingly, more recently in the Falklands war the arguments between Admiral Fieldhouse (Commander-in-Chief Fleet) and Admiral Sir Leach (First Sea Lord) as far as control of the Fleet was concerned had to be resolved at Margaret Thatcher's level. The First Sea Lord was thereafter kept out of the day-to-day operations. Such is the nature of war's nitty-gritty and India was no different. Many false alarms were also raised. Ships at sea reported submarine contacts, and false starts to skirmishes kept everyone in operations rooms on tenterhooks. Submarine crews loaded and unloaded torpedoes and carried out war patrols when not offering anti-submarine warfare practice to ships of the Fleet.

On the Eastern sea-board the newly formed Fleet on 16 October 1971 was also getting into gear for any eventuality. The aircraft carrier Vikrant was handed over to the East. The reasons for doing so will ever be debated. Since nothing succeeds like success and the only enemy submarine in the East, the Ghazi sank too early to cause any damage, the decision has always, in retrospect, been deemed as correct. The Vikrant embarked pilots from all over and worked up the Tigers (300 Seahawk squadron) and the Cobras (310 Alize squadron). As Vizag harbour could not accept the Vikrant the ship perforce had to operate between Madras and deep-water ports off the Andaman Islands. Her movements were classified but she was seen in Madras in August/September, since every year during the monsoons, Madras was her habitat. That year was no different bu thje swords on board were sharper. The ports of Port Blair and Port Cornwallis which offer excellent and deep water for a big ship like the Vikrant saw the ship take respite between flying operations. A letter from Lt Cdr Ashok Sinha, a Seahawk pilot indicated how he was rushed from the Andamans to the carrier for operational duty. He was finding his tour of duty in the Andamans a trifle boring. In a lighter vein now he confides, "It was Yahya Khan who got me transferred out of Port Blair and on to the flat-top and I can't thank him enough."

No wonder the Times of India had the following headlines to sum up the situation on 11 November 1971—"Border Situation Still Grave Says Delhi Spokesman—Pindi Provocation Continues" and another sideline on the front page—"Vital Steps After PM's Return". In fine print the newspapers reported:

With Pakistani troops attempting to intrude into Jammu and Kashmir and their guns continuing to shell posts of Tripura and West Bengal, the situation on Indian borders certainly continues to be grave. The spokesman recalled that Indian troops had instructions not to cross the border and had not done so. For long Pakistan has been describing the Mukti Bahini as Indian agents. Now they have gone a step further. They are describing the forces of the Mukti Bahini as Indian battalions. The report that a submarine had been sighted near Kanya Kumari was without basis, he said. (Surprisingly enough in retrospect this was the PNS Ghazi in transit.) On the subject of vital steps, the first question to be decided by the Political Affairs Committee of the Cabinet on Mrs Gandhi's return from abroad is whether a state of emergency should be declared in view of the grave situation on the eastern border and the increasing intrusions into Jammu and Kashmir. The Defence Minister Mr Jagjivan Ram also toured the Rajasthan border. Emergency was declared in Pakistan on 23 November 1971 and Yahya Khan made that famous remark on 25 November 1971. "In ten days I will not be here—I will be fighting a war." Was this pre-war period an undeclared war? The editorial in the Nepal Times on 30 November 1971 sums up the situation.

Undeclared War

Aerial and tank battles fought by the armies of India and Pakistan have confirmed widespread fears that war is now imminent in the India sub-continent. The world now realizes how close the two countries are to war. The military rulers of Pakistan have even declared that "undeclared war" is going on between the two countries and accordingly proclaimed a state of emergency throughout that country.

The one-sided war waged by the rulers of Pakistan inside what was once a part of their own territory, provoked a resistance which culminated in a well-organized war within a few months. It is thus a war going on inside Bangladesh that is now sought to be described by the Pakistani rulers as an Indo-Pakistan war. In their attempt to project the resistance war inside r as a war between India and Pakistan, they sent their planes and tanks to attack Indian territory. But the planes were shot down and several tanks wee destroyed and much military equipment was captured by the Indian troops. Not even the valuable service rendered by the villain Bhutto, by paying a pilgrimage to Peking, could fully satisfy the military rulers. His desire of being made President or Prime Minister remained unfulfilled. It remains to be seen when Bhutto will outlive his utility.

The Pakistani army has been finding it increasingly difficult to fight its own people. But it wants to be defeated at the hands of a superior power, not at those of the people's resistance movement known as the Mukti Bahini. And for Pakistan, that superior power could be none other than India. Moreover, the military rulers of Pakistan are still obsessed to some extent with their desire of taking revenge for their heavy losses in the 1965 war.

A sensible answer to the question of what should be the attitude of the world towards this strange desire of military rulers of Pakistan, fighting against its own people, can be given only the day when the world is prepared to make an objective analysis of events which have taken place in Pakistan during the past one year. The military regime of Pakistan has been conducting an undeclared war against its own people, a war of mercilessly suppressing the right, life and property of its people. The world has to direct its appeal for disengagement from this war and restraint towards Pakistan, not to any third country. The intentions of those who try to teach a lesson of restraint to India, which has displayed unparalleled fortitude of enduring an invasion which has been mounted on it by ten million refugees, are doubtful.

What Next?

With such worked-up state of the Naval Fleets no one knew the place, date and time when they could be called into action. Tensions ran high, and surprisingly anyone being transferred out of a Fleet ship resented the move. At times life seemed normal and yet one sensed war was round the corner. It is well known that in end November 1971 the fine and outstanding aviator Capt R.H. Tahiliani, commanding INS Trishul and Captain F 15 (now Admiral and Chief of the Naval Staff) broke his ankle whilst riding a horse on the Colaba Golf Course in the company of his Fleet

Commander Rear Admiral Chandy Kuruvilla. Though the Captain was transferred out much to his chagrin, Capt K.M.V Nair, popularly known as Curly took over as F 15 and a perfectly tuned and worked up INS Trishul and Talwar (Cdr S.S. Kumar). Both these ships went on to win Vir Chakras for their captains in their heroic actions off Karachi in support of the missile boat attacks on 9 December 1971, described in the relevant chapter.

The three services in particular and the nation in general sensed the scare of war in the air. In every such situation contingency plans, strategic and tactical planning and battle readiness come to the fore. A small but determined Indian Navy was seen more often at sea preparing for the worst. Wives and children saw less of their husbands and fathers. Refit schedules of ships were stepped up and the dockyards began to work with fervour never seen before. Battle drills attained extreme seriousness. The level of efficiency that was passable in peacetime was not acceptable at this juncture, and officers and men were goaded to give of their best. Co-operation and a thrust for improved levels of battle fitness automatically rose. Peacetime drills and ceremonials took second place and the man in uniform and the civilian worker in the dockyard co-operated to achieve new heights. The standard of security improved and both shore office and store organizations which sometimes stagnate in peacetime, rose to the occasion. Staff support and supply positions were favourably improved for the benefit of the Fleet.

All this happened without much goading from higher quarters. Understandably Naval Headquarters also did their homework earnestly. Understanding between the three Service Chiefs, General S.H.F. Manekshaw (now Field Marshal), Late Air Chief Marshal P.C. Lal and Admiral S.M. Nanda improved. Their co-operation was later to see heights of glory. The Defence Ministry also shed some of its bureaucratic ways and financial powers were delegated to the Services, as a one-time measure. All these apparently normal measures were to pay rich dividends in December. This was the time to sharpen one's sword, oil the barrel, warm the bell, sponge out the gun and to be ready for war. As Gen Renhard Gehlen of the German Intelligence predicted the happenings of World War II to Hitler by gleaning media reports intelligently a discerning professional could do likewise by reading the following samples.

PRESS REPORT ON PRESIDENT YAHYA KHAN'S INTERVIEW WITH BBC

"If fighting continues along the border between East Pakistan and India, it may lead to war."

"I cannot just tell my army to stop it and take it. For the defence of the country, I will not turn the other cheek. I will hit back."

Pakistan Times, Lahore, 2 August 1971

STATEMENT BY Z.A. BHUTTO, CHAIRMAN, PPP (23 SEPTEMBER 1971)

Mr Z.A. Bhutto, Chairman PPP said: "PPP would extend whole hearted co-operation to crush the Indian aggression".
—Pakistan Times, Lahore, 24 September 1971

SPEECH OF LT. GEN. (RETD) BAKHTIAR RANA (23 SEPTEMBER 1971)

Lt Gen (Retd) Bakhtiar Rana, addressing a meeting, said:
"India, in spite of her military superiority, can never defeat Pakistan. If we remain united, India will get another crushing defeat."
—Imroze, Lahore, 24 September 1971

PRESIDENT YAHAY KHAN'S INTERVIEW WITH THE NEWSWEEK MAGAZINE (USA)

"…I have no reason to tell you war is not imminent because it is …If the Indians escalate with a view to capturing territory and installing a puppet Bangladesh regime, that will be war…
—Newsweek magazine, 8 November 1971

PRESIDENT YAHYA KHAN TALKING TO PAKISTAN TROOPS IN SIALKOT AREA (12 NOVEMBER 1971)

"…If a war, in spite of our best efforts to avoid it, is thrust on us, the valiant armed forces of Pakistan—who repose their trust in the strength of their faith and the help of Allah more than anything else—will defend every inch of their sacred soil and crush the aggressor."
Morning News, Karachi, 13 November 1971

PRESIDENT YAHYA KHAN'S STATEMENT AS REPORTED BY A.P. (25 NOVEMBER 1971)

"In ten days, I might not be here in Rawalpindi. I will be fighting a war."

—AP, 25 November 1971

DAY BY DAY ACCOUNT OF THE WAR

Slowly but surely came the call:
The sudden war surprised us all;
Hard was the trial, but why complain
We trust to do it, if called again,
Many gallant lives came to an end
They died, as they lived, as everyone's friend;
But for the dead parting came suddenly
One was never able to say good bye.
       —*Dedicated to those who gave up their lives.*

The clashes between the Indian and Pakistani forces on the East Pakistan border had been going on since 21 November 1971 and on 3 December culminated into an open war when the Pakistan Air Force made surprise attacks on Indian targets. This chapter is a brief description of the 14-day war which ended with the Pakistani forces surrendering in the East on 16 December. The unilateral cease-fire by India and its acceptance by Pakistani Yahya Khan and the reasons for India's success are discussed in later chapters. The events of those 14 fateful days had historical and geographical repercussions, and were intended by India to thwart the evil designs of the military rulers of Pakistan. Much bloodshed could have been avoided if Pakistan had made genuine efforts to arrive at a political solution in its eastern wing. In the final analysis, the war is a pointer for India and Pakistan to seek closer ties and understanding to avoid another 1971.

3 December (Friday)—The First Day

Dawn broke on 3 December like any other, with high tension in the air. The end of the day witnessed the beginning of a new chapter in Indian history. Pakistani Air Force fighters struck at seven major air fields— Srinagar, Avantipur (Kashmir), Amritsar, Pathankot, Ambala (Punjab) Barmer and Jodhpur (Rajasthan)—between 1740 and 1810 hours just after dusk, hoping to cripple the Indian Air Force on the ground. But the Indian aircraft had been well dispersed, and only a little damage was caused. At 1830 hours the Pakistani armoured forces and infantry crossed the cease-fire line in Kashmir in the Poonch sector and 11 border posts in Kashmir and Punjab were heavily shelled.

As Keesing's Archives puts it, Pakistan had four main aims:
(1) to reduce the pressure on the forces in East Pakistan by creating a diversion in the West; (2) to occupy territories in Kashmir and Rajasthan;

(3) to bargain terms of settlement in the East; and (4) to secure intervention of the great powers or the United Nations. The timing of the attack is attributed to the following factors:

—Bombing operations on 3 December would be facilitated by a full moon.
—Attack by Muslims on Friday, their Sabbath, would surprise India.
—If operations in Kashmir were delayed, snow would cause hindrance.

Pakistan sought to convince the world that the Indian Army had launched an offensive between 3.30 and 4 pm, but could not prove it. As the Prime Minister, Defence Minister and Finance Minister were out of Delhi at the time, the reply to the Pakistani attack took time. At 11 pm President Giri signed the proclamation of Emergency.

A war telegram of sorts was released from Delhi indicating the Emergency and the three Services went into action, for the very contingency for which the armed forces had been preparing. Lady Luck smiled on the Indian Navy because the majority of her Eastern and Western Fleet ships were out at sea on manoeuvres on that fateful day. This was fortunate, for during such pre-emptive attacks, ships in harbour are very vulnerable.

Eight days earlier President Yahya Khan had indicated very strongly a threat of war with India. The Services, and particularly the Indian Navy, were certainly ready.

Naval bases were put on alert, the war room at Naval Headquarters and Maritime Operation rooms at Bombay, Cochin, Visakhapatnam, Okha, Madras and Calcutta were activated with commanders and their staffs in attendance. Defensive measures against pre-emptive underwater attacks, control of merchant shipping and dowsing of navigational lights were promptly ordered. The nation was glued to the radio sets and awaited the important announcement that Mrs. Gandhi made just after midnight:

"I speak to you at a moment of grave peril to our country and to our people. Some hours ago, soon after 5.30 p.m. on December 3, Pakistan launched a full-scale war against us. The Pakistan Air Force suddenly struck at our airfields in Amritsar, Pathankot, Srinagar, Uttarlai, Jodhpur, Ambala and Agra. Their ground forces are shelling our defence positions in Sulaimanki, Khem Karan, Poonch and other sectors.

Since last March, we have borne the heaviest burden and withstood the greatest pressure, in a tremendous effort to urge the world to help in bringing about a peaceful solution and preventing the annihilation of an entire people, whose only crime was to vote for democracy. But the world ignored the basic causes and concerned itself only with certain repercussions.

The situation was bound to deteriorate and the courageous band of freedom-fighters have been staking their all in defence of the values for which we also have struggled, and which are basic to our way of life.

Today, the war in Bangladesh has become a war on India. This has imposed upon me, my Government and the people of India a great responsibility. We have no other option but to put our country on a war footing. Our brave officers and jawans are at their post mobilized for the defence of the country. An Emergency has been declared for the whole of India. Every necessary step is being taken, and we are prepared for all eventualities.

I have no doubt that it is the united will of our people that the wanton and unprovoked aggression should be decisively and finally repelled. In this resolve, the Government is assured of the full and unflinching support of all political parties and every Indian citizen. We must be prepared for a long period of hardship and sacrifice.

We are a peace-loving people. But we know that peace cannot last if we do not guard our democracy and our way of life. So today, we fight not merely for territorial integrity but for the basic ideals which have given strength to this country and on which alone we can progress to a better future.

Aggression must be met, and the people of India will meet it with fortitude and determination and with discipline and utmost unity.

Jai Hind!"

The Prime Minister spoke in a voice charged with little emotion and more grit. It gave men at sea that feeling of wanting to do their best for their country. To the older generation at sea their Prime Minister's speech reminded one of Sir Winston Churchill's famous speech at the outbreak of World War II. In 1939, when England went to war with Germany he warned the nation of ups and downs but with a prediction of ultimate victory all of which came true.

Civil defence measures of blackout and regulation of night traffic came into effect and India was at war with Pakistan on the Bangla issue, even though open words of declaration of war came to know of the PAF attacks and altered many of the local Service Commanders that evening.

In the Bay of Bengal

The Eastern Fleet consisted of the Vikrant (Flag R Adm S.H. Sarma, Captain S. Prakash), the Brahmaputra (Capt J.C. Puri), the Beas (Cdr L. Ramdas), the Kamorta (Capt M.P. Awati, P31), the Kavaratti (Cdr Subir Paul). These ships were somewhere in the Bay of Bengal and were nominated as the 'Strike task' group. The submarine Khanderi (Cdr R.J. Millan) formed the subsurface force and Landing Ship Tank Craft Magar (Cdr T.N. Singhal) Gharial (Lt. Cdr A.K. Sharma) and Guldar (Lt. Cdr U. Dabir) were nominated for transportation and amphibious role. The Rajput (Lt Cdr Inder Singh), Panvel (Lt Cdr J.P.A. Naronha), Pulicat (Lt S. Krishnan) and Akshay (Lt. S.D. More) were the local Defence group with Desh Deep, the light vessel tender being requisitioned and commissioned for afloat support. They all received the famous flash signal from their Commander-in-Chief:

```
FM    FOCINC EAST    —Flash—
TO    S/A Keeping IV Series
      Commence Hostilities Against Pakistan
```

The Fleet Commander and Commanding Officers opened their sealed orders, rehearsed battle drills earnestly, briefed their command teams and spoke to their men for that ultimate in Command—drive your ship to near death, deliver deadly blows and come away if you can, unscathed. It was near midnight when INS Rajput sighted a suspicious disturbance resembling a periscope whilst on patrol off Visakhapatnam and attacked the spot with depth charges. A loud under-water explosion followed, which was heard and experienced by the coastal residents of Visakhapatnam, accompanied by a flash from the disturbed sea. The ship continued with her mission little realizing that her depth-charge attack had in some way led to the destruction of PNS Ghazi, which was to be severe and demoralizing blow to the Pakistan Navy and that nation. The carrier Vikrant was away, but Admiral Krishnan had made some ruses to indicate that the big flat-top was off Visakhapatnam and proceeding to Madras. The Ghazi had been told to lie in wait for the prized carrier and fell prey to a watery grave herself. The entire story is given in a later chapter.

The arming policy was upgraded and ships companies were busy fuzing shells in magazines. Many a young heart must have beat harder as this oft taught drill which is sparingly executed in peacetime, was now conducted on the full war ammunition outfit of a ship. Accidents can take place, if one is not careful.

In the West

The Western Fleet with the more powerful missile-fitted units was in readiness and 3 December saw most of its units at sea, having sailed out for a sortie on 2 December. The aims of the Western Fleet were clearly to deliver a blow to enemy ships and installations; to defend our own coast and shipping. To do this task, the Fleet and missile units had exercised regularly and had only returned to harbour on 30 November. The line-up to undertake the task at sea lay on the Mysore (Flag R Adm E.C. Kuruvilla, Capt R.K.S. Gandhi), the Trishul (F 15 Capt K.M.V. Nair), Talwar (Cdr S.S. Kumar), the Khukri (F 14 Capt M.N. Mulla), the Kuthar (Cdr U.C. Tripathi), the Kirpan (Cdr R.R. Sood) Kiltan (Capt Gopal Rao) Katchall (Cdr K.N. Zadu) Kadmatt (Cdr S. Jain) and eight new missile boats of the Osa class (K 25 Cdr B.B. Yadav), the recently acquired from the USSR and completely manned by the Indian Navy—dispelling all foreign reports that Russians were on board. The fleet support tanker Deepak (Capt. P.C. Andrews) had order to rendezvous ships and feed oil to the Fleet. The submarines Karanj (Cdr V.S. Shekhawat), and the Kurusura (Cdr A. Auditto), were in readiness for patrols and one of them was at sea waiting to kill but with strict orders of positive identification of Pakistani warships before attacking. This, in any war, is a tall order and hampers a submarine Commander's initiative in otherwise unrestricted warfare. A host of other ships and mine-sweepers in the order of battle were also ready to go wherever ordered.

The South

The ships of the Southern flotilla comprising the Amba (Cdr V.A. Dhareshwar), the Ganga (Lt Cdr S.K. Kulshrestha) and the Godawari (Cdr H.D. Singh) were sailed with orders to intercept Pakistani merchant ships. They patrolled off choke points. As there was no Fleet Commander at sea, the operations were independent and monitored by the Flag Officer Southern Naval Area, Rear Admiral V.A. Kamath.

4 December 71—the Second Day
The fear of outside intervention was high. India invoked the relevant acts of the Indo-Soviet Treaty of Peace, Friendship and Co-operation which provided for consultation in the event of an attack or threatened attack upon either party. This was possibly a good insurance against China.

The second day of war should generally have been one of chaos with the Army and the Air Force settling down but it was not so. The nation's defence forces had retaliated in unison. The Indian Air Force downed 33 Pakistani Air Force planes, attacked enemy tanks and forward positions, whilst the Army moved east into Bangladesh, and held the Pakistani Army at bay. The Defence of India Bill was passed and wide-ranging powers were issued to the Defence Ministry and subordinate commanders. In the Ferozepore sector, one Pak enemy brigade of IV Corps (Lt Gen Bahadur Sher) supported by air, armour and artillery attacked the Indian position near Hussainiwala. The enemy was repulsed with casualties. An attack on Chhamb by I Corps of Pakistan (Lt Gen Khan Irshad) was contained. The declaration of war by Pakistan was made official and all service-men in Pakistan and persons under 60 years of age were called up to be ready to serve. President Yahya Khan went on the air to exhort his nation to "march forward and give the hardest blow of Allah Ho Akbar to the enemy. God is with us", he said, "Pakistan Zindabad". He emphatically stated that "we are at war with a cunning and cruel enemy. Our brave awns have torn the enemy to pieces by attacking it in the 1965 war. This time God willing, we shall strike the enemy harder than before.

In the Bay

The pet name tigers is given to the Jet Squadron INAS 300 based on the Vikrant and its pilots used to fly the British built Seahawks with the ferocious White Tiger painted across each flying machine. The term "Cobras' is given to the French built Alize Squadron INAS 310 also based on the Vikrant capable of ground attack and anti-submarine warfare missions. These two Squadrons were commissioned in 1960 in the U.K. and France by then Cdr (P) R.H. Tahiliani the White tiger and Cdr (O) M.K. Roy the Cobra respectively. Both had since left the action to a younger lot who now came into their own. The tiger squadron was commanded by Lt Cdr S. Gupta, whilst the Cobras were led by the late Lt Cdr Ravi Dhit. Both were ready for action, something they had been waiting for long—the Tigers to kill and the Cobras to bite. The early hours of 4 December saw the Vikrant scouring the seas off Cox's Bazar; the mission was cleared with briefings to strike airfields, fuel dumps, installations and to deny their use to the enemy at Cox's Bazar.

The first sortie of 8 Seahawks catapulted and screamed off the deck at about 1100—destination Cox's Bazar airfield. The first sortie drew blood and a bevy of the finest pilots who had been commissioned in U.K. Under Tahiliani were in the foray to be led by Gigi Gupta, Gulab Israni, Ash Sinha, Fido Sharma and A.K. Mehra as section leaders. The anti-aircraft gunfire was braved and much damage done to the airfield. A hero's welcome awaited the return of the flight and when the fighter controller reported all eight contacts on the radar screen, the ship's company of INS Vikrant went mad with cheer and happiness and received their pilots, the day's bread winners, with affection. They then began to turn around and re-arm their aircraft. A proud C-in-C East had the following message for the two arm commanders:

Personal for GOC-in-C East (Lt Gen Aurora) and AOC-in-C East (Air Marshal Dewan (.) Cox's Bazar attacked by eight aircraft (.) All aircraft returned safely (.) Result of strike, rocket and strafing (.) All airfield installations destroyed (.) air Traffic Control on fire (.) Power house and wireless station severely damaged (.) Fuel dump ablaze (.)

There was no respite on board the Vikrant for the ground crew or the White Tigers. Shortly after noon, the Seahawks were screaming away again this time to wreck the well-fortified Chittagong airfield. The reception was hot from medium-to heavy anti-aircraft gun-fire. The bleeding kills that followed gave the results of one harbour and control tower damaged, fuel dump set ablaze, two gunboats immobilized, six Pakistani merchant ships attacked in outer anchorage, and two damaged heavily. All but one of the Vikrant's birds returned to mother safely, which having been hit by anti-aircraft fire, was repaired quickly. It was victory all round and the enemy made the following signal:

> From: Fleet Cdr East Fleet To DFNX
> Chittagong harbour and base under heavy air attack.

While the Tigers were digesting their kill, the Cobras, slowly but surely w ere launched at night to raid the enemy and to give him no respite. It was 4 December that saw the Vikrant's finest hours, the pilots ably supported by her 1200 ships crew writing history with bravery and the magnificent achievements of that day. Cdr H.M.L. Saxena (later DNO) the ship's commander, pepped up the men. Cdr Bilo Choudhry, the tough straight-talking engineer, (now with ONGC as a Member) kept the boilers and engines full steam ahead despite problems. There was no rest for anyone on that ship but only short catnaps and shut eyes, to be ready to keet up the pressure on East Pakistani airfields.

The escorts Brahmputra (Capt J.C. Puri) and Beas (Cdr L. Ramdas) were in company of the Vikrant (Capt S. Pariahs) had their share of excitement when they attacked, what they thought was submarine sighted by them. This was reported in the Press the next day. Lieut. D' Silva and sub-Lieut Hukku saw a periscope and 4.5" guns also opened up on the contact and a kill was claimed. This target which was possibly a false contact was similar to incidents to be repeated in the Falklands War. Sub and non-sub-contacts were attacked many times. Interestingly this Press report of a submarine kill in the East on 4 December, declared much later, got mixed up with that of PNS Ghazi which was sunk and the matter closed. It was indeed a red-letter day for the Eastern Naval Command. Morale was high, since the Fleet ships had assumed that they had killed a sub-marine and the fliers had created havoc ashore.

In the words of Eastern Naval News January 1972 the supposed submarine action on 4 December 1971 is described thus:

This was no all on this momentous day. One of the screen ships of Vikrant picked up a submarine contact at about 1330 hrs on 4 December 1971 and carried out prompt attacks with mortars. Soon other escorts joined the fray and subsequent deliberate attacks compelled the submarine to break surface. Apparently she had lost control and was coming up fast at a steep angle, the bow and part of the fin breaking surface in a flurry of frothy water and spray. She appeared to be desperate and fired a couple of torpedoes all of which went wide of their mark. Our stout-hearted ships at once presented her a few 4.5" shells which were caught on her casing. Alizes also joined the fray and the sub had a good taste of their depth charge with a loud flash. The submarine was seen diving—or was she dying?—never to surface again, nor to be heard of again.'

In the West

The Western Fleet was at sea ready for battle. Apparently the Pakistani Fleet failed to come out which confused the Indian Fleet commander, Chandy Kuruvilla. The C-in-C West (Vice Adm S.N. Kohli) must have just then opened his orders and set in motion the attack on Karachi, hoping his fleet would be already on its way. The Western Fleet should have been going towards Karachi, but the Fleet seemed to get sidetracked into intercepting merchant ships and began a hunt for the Pakistani Fleet. Hence the Kiltan (Cdr Gopal Rao) for Command and Control and the Katchall (Cdr K.N. Zadu) were ordered to meet up the Nirghat (Lt Cdr I.J. Sharma), Nipat (Cdr Babru Yadav, K-25), Lt Cdr B.N. Kavina) and Veer (Lt Cdr O.P. Mehta) and were put on their way to Karachi under shore control. The C-in-C was seen in the Maritime Operations Room, fingers crossed, having let his killer dogs loose on Karachi with no air cover. The soviets had treated these small 80-ton craft as shore defence vessels and never as attack craft, always to be used for close-range defence from home ports. Many are the restrictions on fuel, speed and sea states: yet all were intelligently dealt with by superior planning. With speeds in excess of 28 knots, the small boats, which offer minimum radar targets, approached Karachi in darkness, launched their Styx missiles on the enemy positions and ships. Pakistani officers on duty in the control room at Karachi failed to realize that it was a seaborne attack. Assuming it was an air attack the Pak defences were confused, mesmerized and utterly in disarray to arrange for seaward defence. The missile boats who themselves were worked up and full of excitement, were relieved to be allowed their goal without retaliation, and happily retired to head for home with a few missiles still intact for their retiring phase. What a successful sortie these well trained officers had, and the newspapers of India were all praise for the attack. Keesing's Archives reporting the incident in January 1972 had this to say:

In the biggest naval battle since the Second World War an Indian Task Force sank the Pakistani destroyers Khaibar (formerly HMS Cadiz and Shah Jahan (formerly HMS Charity) and two mine sweepers off Karachi in the early hours of 5 December and subsequently shelled naval installations in the port. (In actual fact only PNS Khaibar sank) (Capt Nasseem Mallik was in command).

The mine sweeper has been identified as PNS Muhafiz. The historic attack is commemorated as Navy day. All Commanding Officers were decorated for their heroic sortie. Which will long be remembered for it earned the Navy two MVCs and 4 VrCs.

Message from Chief of Naval Staff

The signal message from the Chief released at the outbreak of hostilities was clear:

Pakistan has committed an unprovoked aggression against us and our defence services have been ordered to meet this challenge with full courage and determination. My objective is to seek and destroy Pakistani lines of communication and along with the sister services; inflict the maximum damage on the enemy war machine.

I expect all officers, sailors and civilians in the Navy to do their duty and act according to the best traditions of our great Service. No sacrifice should be too much for us. Let us write a new and glorious chapter in the history of our Service.

How confident Nanda was that the Indian Navy would write a new chapter is abundantly clear from his message. By the evening of 5 December a sense of pride filled each operational and support man of the Navy to set forth for greater glory.

How the Media Saw It

A four-column report in the Bombay edition of the times of India (6 December) quoting a Western Naval Command spokesman said:

An Indian Naval Task Force inflicted a crippling blow on the Pakistani Navy, sinking two destroyers and damaging another in a surprise attack on Karachi in the early hours of Sunday.

Units of the task force then went as close as 25 kilometers of Karachi harbour and shelled several strategic installations.

A spokesman of the Western Naval Command said in Bombay the two enemy destroyers sunk were believed to be the Khaibar and the Shah Jahan.

Not one of the Indian units attacking Karachi received the slightest damage in the first major naval battle fought by the Indian Navy since independence. What largely contributed to the big victory was the "daring and perfectly timed action" of the units of the Western Naval command, the spokesman said.

The losses suffered by it in Sunday's battle, it is believed will have a crippling effect on the enemy navy as its effective strength is known to comprise only seven destroyers and a cruiser. Two of the destroyers had been converted some time ago into anti-submarine frigates.

The naval spokesman said Karachi was a heavily defended harbour with highly sophisticated guns, radar and missiles. The Karachi area was also known to have strong air defence cover, particularly guarding maritime targets.

The harbour was also protected by a ring of ships and Pakistan had boasted that no enemy ship could approach the harbour closer than 100 kilometers, the spokesman added.

The Western Naval command had taken all this into account in planning an carrying out the daring attack on Karachi without any air support.

The surface action by our task force began shortly past midnight on Saturday and lasted an hour.

As the Indian naval units steamed towards Karachi the radar showed the approaches protected by four ships on the outer patrol about 50 kilometers from the shore.

The naval spokesman said it would take possibly a day more to give a detailed account of the battle as the ship-to-shore wireless contact had been suspended for tactical reasons.

The information gathered so far had been through certain signals put out by the units which went into action.

Possibly one more ship had been hit and it had been seen turning back into the harbour. The Khaibar class destroyers carry a complement of 300 men and Shahjahan 250.

"Independent observers with long enough memories have compared the operations of 5 December with the sinking of British warships, Prince of Wales and Repulse by the Japanese off Singapore in 1941. the two fleets of the Indian Navy have bagged more than two warships but the kill is not as important as the element of surprise involved in the operations and the sense of shock it must have caused to the enemy. It was about 6 pm on December 3, 1971, that Pakistan unleashed war on India with a surprise air attack on several of our airfields. Nearly six hours later India decided to hit back. And within twenty-four hours a task force of our Western Fleet accomplished a veritable feat off Karachi", said another report.

"Karachi in the west was the obvious target for isolation because it was the home of the bulk of the surface ships of the Pakistan Navy. Therefore, talking the Pakistani pre-emptive strike of 3 December as the signal the Western Naval Command got ready to tackle the enemy at its strongest point", commented the Indian Express.

About the Navy's action in the East, quoting a message received at the Eastern Naval Command Headquarters in Visakhapatnam a PTI report on

4 December said:

Chittagong harbour was seen ablaze as ships and aircraft of the Eastern Naval Fleet bombed and rocketed it today...

Not a single vessel could hereafter be put to sea from Chittagong, the message said, adding that several direct hits were made on its headquarters complex as well as transit camps and enemy fuel tanks.

The enemy had been caught in a pincer movement...

Cox's Bazar port was also hit and the Eastern Fleet continued to maintain pressure on the two ports throughout the day...

5/6 December—The Third Day

The battle ground was now fully in East Pakistan and the "Mukti Bahini" forces moved in complete concert with the Indian Army in the East and liberated areas in Bangladesh and entered Balmonirghat. The Soviet Union vetoed the Security Council resolution for an immediate cease-fire on the ground that it placed Indian and Pakistan on the same footing, though Pakistan was the aggressor. So the war was to go on. General Aurora continued his encircling move and Fenni fell (See map). The scene in the west where the land battle was being fought was a cause for concern. Pakistan had launched a major infantry attack, supported by armour at Longanwala. This attack was repulsed with close IAF air support. On the night of 5/6 December approximately two brigades of Pakistani troops, supported by an armour regiment, attacked Indian positions twice in the Chhamb sector. Both attacks were being repulsed but Chhamb area was to be the scene of fierce fighting and tank battles with a lot of ups and downs, which indeed is what war is all about. The army advanced into the Sialkot sector, engaged in a tank battle in the Khem Karan sector and captured Chadbet in the Kutch in a pre-dawn attack.

In the Bay

The Vikrant was now mounting sortie after sortie. Areas to the west of Khulna, Mongla and Chalna saw naval aerial attacks and a warning was issued that only a white flag would save lives on ships and shore bases. The Chief of the Naval Staff was pleased with the progress of the war and made the famous signal to the Navy.

"Personal from CNS (.) Good shooting, well done.

Hit hard and keep on hitting."

FOCINC EAST, not to be outdone, made a brief message to his Command, "From C-in-C (.) Motto for Eastern Fleet is "Attack, Attack, Attack."

As the carrier pilots gained combat experience and confidence, they were seen to choose targets carefully for the balance to be in their favour. At Mongla, the air-strike was received with heavy anti-aircraft fire from gun positions on river banks, and from anti-aircraft guns mounted on Pak gunboats. Two gun boats were silenced and heavy strafing was attempted wherever gunfire emanated. At Khulna, anti-aircraft fire spat forth from batteries and from the merchant ships, which had to be silenced. On the Pussur River, which is a tributary of the Ganges, the port wireless station, the lifeline for Pakistan naval communications was put out of action and when the merchant ship Ondarda spat anti-aircraft fire, the Seahawks went for her and sent her to the bottom of the sea with their rocket attacks. Once again all aircraft returned safely. Between the ships making a ring at sea and air strikes mounted with precision, the blockade of the East was complete. That morning's briefing (possibly) gave Mrs. Gandhi confidence to recognize "Ganga Praja Tantri Bangladesh" which she declared in the Lok Sabha adding "Our thoughts at this moment are with the father of this State (Mujibur Rahman).

6 December saw the pilots divert attention to Chittagong on request from the IAF. The Seahawks went in by day and pounded the strong bastion of the enemy. The army barracks and the workshops went up in flames and the Patenga battery which comprised 12 to 15 anti-aircraft guns was silenced, and an armed merchant ship struck. The 'Tigers' rested after dusk and the 'Cobras' went in by night. Though the city was blacked out, the light of a steel mill helped navigation towards the airport which was successfully bombed and craters reported. After all, their C-in-C Krishnan had said in no uncertain terms, "Attack, Attack, Attack.

The coordination between the three C-in-Cs had been excellent. A signal from AOC-in-C East Air Marshal Dewan testifies to this:

"Personal (.) Extremely happy to hear good work done by your boys (.) Request you search for grass landing strips in your area of responsibility and render them unusable (.) Also suggest you neutralize runways in Chittagong and Cox's Bazar area, both by bombardment and airstrikes."

In the West and South

The Fleet was all over attempting to meet set rendezvous and intercepting merchant ships. The Fleet Commander came to know of the successful attack on Karachi and newspaper cuttings with the headline sum up the mood of the moment. Merchant ships were being re-routed and in the south, the Godavari was busy rounding up the Pakistan vessel MV Pasni. Possibly an Indian Navy submarine was in wait off the Pakistan coast outside of the Indian Navy's proposed tracks to Karachi, but no Pakistan Navy ships came out to seek battle.

How the Media Saw It

A PTI dispatch from Colombo quoting the then Ceylon Broadcasting Corporation said:
All Pakistani international flights operating through Colombo have been suspended until further notice.

The CBC made the announcement in this morning's news bulletin and added that, in view of the current situation in the Indian sub-continent Pakistani long-distance flights had been diverted to Katunayake international airport for refueling...
The CBC's announcement implies that PIA's commercial flights between the two wings of Pakistan via Colombo have been suspended and flights to other parts of the world, like the Canton halt at Colombo, allowed only for refueling without taking or disembarking passengers...
Ceylon in recent days, has repeatedly affirmed that no military hardware or army personnel will be allowed to be carried by Pakistani military planes touching Ceylon for refueling and every plane is being checked by the Ceylonese authorities.

— "Bhuj, Okha port bombed" The Times of India reported on 5 December from Ahmedabad: "Pakistani aircraft intruded into Bhuj at 4.55 a.m. and dropped two bombs. No damage was done. Five enemy planes dropped two bombs on Okha port at 7.30 p.m. when Cdr Khambatta and his men heroically fought an oil fire.
— Lt Col Baig commanding 25 Frontier Force surrendered at Comilla with 8 JCO's and 235 men.

6/7 December—The Fifth Day

This was a day of political activity and a lull in naval operations. Harold Wilson, former British Prime Minister said in an interview to the Times of India that the American statement supporting Pakistan was 'stupid and ill considered". A news item also hinted that Nixon might visit Pakistan enroute to china. Thirty Members of Parliament of various political parties protested outside the US Embassy in Delhi.
The Chief of Staff of the Pakistan Army meanwhile told General Niazi who was leading the forces in East Pakistan, that there was every hope of Chinese activity soon. The Pakistani author who asserts this says there was no basis for such expectation, but General Niazi kept pestering the high command, for his position was beginning to look forlorn.

On 7 December Jessore cantonment was occupied by the Indians as 107 Brigade withdrew towards Khulna. This again was an indicator that the rout of the Pakistan Army had begun. Once again General Khan, the Pakistani author is clear and writes:

Lt General Niazi, who had lost the war in his mind by December 6 had by December 10 given up all hope of any help from outside. In fact later when General Farman Ali had sounded Soviet, British, French and U.S. representatives in Dacca to take control of East Pakistan, General Niazi and Admiral Sharif had agreed. When Farman Ali's statement was countermanded by Yahya Khan, he requested that either he be allowed to make statements or face a court martial to vindicate his honour.

The state of East Pakistan was one of collapse even as only four days of the war had elapsed. An interesting incident is reported in the Keesing's Archives: A UN aircraft was cleared to proceed to Bangladesh to evacuate casualties and when the aircraft approached the coast it came within a few miles of the Vikrant. The news of this neutral flight was not made known to the Navy. The Vikrant opened up its entire anti-aircraft wrath and the aircraft flew back to Calcutta. It possibly showed the Vikrant was on the ball, but not our lines of communication with the UN. The next day the flight went off as planned with better lines of communication and the UN Markings were clearly identified.

How the Media Saw It

The Army's progress in the East was reported by PTI from Calcutta, where chief of Staff Eastern Command Maj. Gen. J.F.R. Jacob addressed a Press conference on the morning of 7 December:

The Indian Army today entered Jessore airfield.

Fighting was now in progress to clear Jessore cantonment and town. Simultaneously, the Indian troops made a big thrust from Bongaon Road and liberated Sirsa...

Fighting was now going on around the town of Dinapur in the north... Operations were now in progress to clear Jamalpur town to Mymensingh Sector...

In the Sylhet Sector, Sunamganj town has been taken.

Comilla cantonment and town had been surrounded from all sides and now remained isolated.

A naval citation read:

Cox's Bazar was the main target on December 7. There was perfect division of labour, with the Seahawks (endearingly called White Tigers)...concentrating on the airfield and the Alizes, otherwise known as Cobras, preferring fuel dumps. Our pilots then headed for Chittagong;

Patenga battery did not open up as usual. However, not to leave things to chance the Seahawks carried out rocketing raids at the Patenga point. Complete silence from the battery indicated that the earlier raids had done their work.

That evening returning home to the mother ship our fliers saw the first sign of impending Pakistani surrender. Pakistani craft off Chittagong and in Cox's Bazar were flying large white flags from the highest point on their masts.

The fleet was now ideally placed for a strike on Barisal where enemy troop concentration was reported. The Alizes, therefore, carried out a night attack under moonlight confitions. No ship movements were observed in the Tetulia, Bighai and Bishakali rivers in the Barisal area during this attack. But the Seahawks in the next wave of attack on the Barisal, Bakarganj and Patuakhali areas sighted and destroyed three enemy barges laden with troops, arms and equipment.

A UNI correspondent who visited Indian-occupied Dera Baba Nanak on 8 December wrote:

Dera Baba Nanak proved the dead-end for the Pakistanis. Retreating, they left their dead behind. The momentous task accomplished by or troops in a four-hour lightning action on Tuesday morning (7 December) is difficult to describe. One has to see it for oneself. Our troops drove out the enemy from well-entrenched positions. In these areas, they hold 60 square km of Pakistani territory. Thirty two Pakistani soldiers were captured and several were killed. We are watching them being buried. The captured arms and ammunition included Chinese made anti-tanki guns, rifles and recoilless guns with American markings. It was in a jeep left behind by fleeing Pakistanis that the journalist went to the area.

8/9 December—The Seventh Day

The political news of the day was disturbing. The UN resolution that had been vetoed in the Security Council was tabled again. The UN General Assembly voted upon a resolution calling upon Indian and Pakistan to cease-fire immediately and withdraw armed forces to their own, territories. India's stand was unambiguous, that no cease-fire could come about without a free Bangladesh to enable return of the refugees. It was surprising to learn that Sadat's Egypt and Bandaranaike's Ceylon voted with USA and China, whilst Britain and France displayed some conscience by abstaining. The war to liberated East Bengal continued unabated. The United Nations yet proved to be a strange place. Ceylon (now Sri Lanka) voted for the pro-Pak resolution on the plea that a future danger to Sri Lanka's territorial integrity existed on account of the minority problem of the Tamils: how right their premonitions have come to pass. Some nations generously voted with the proviso that if there is war, shooting must stop first. Thus, humanitarian concern mingled with the insistence of some countries that domestic aspect of repression is sacrosanct, giving Nixon a lever to support Yahya Khan.

The Army's advance into Bangladesh continued with high tempo ensuring the liberation of Comilla, Bramanbaria, Chandpur and Dandkandi. Newspaper headlines reported the enemy on the run in Bangladesh and a bridge-head on Meghna River was established (See map).

The Chhamb Sector in the West saw the Pakistanis mounting a fierce attack with an additional brigade heavily supported by armour and air cover. Indian troops held their ground, but just so. The western bank of Munawar Tawi was occupied, advance into Sialkot sector by six kilometers was also reported. Naushera was raided and an attack in Dera Baba Nanak was repulsed. Five posts in Kargil were captured, whilst there was little or no news from the Poonch Sector. Flight Lieutenant Wazir Ali Khan piloting a MIG-19 was shot down and Lt Gulam Mohamed of 19th Punjab taken prisoner.

In the Bay

Air strikes continued to show their results. The Eastern Fleet, heralded by the Vikrant and other ships, was in full command of the seas and surrounding air spaces. The Pakistani Air Force in the East had been written off except for remnants as indicated by AOC-in-C Eastern Command late on 7 December—"I am convinced the remains of Pakistan Air Force in Bangladesh are operating from Cox's Bazar and Chittagong. Today army position was engaged by Sabre jets in Agartala area twice at different times. You make all runways unfit for operation in your area of responsibility by heavy bombardment/air effort." This amounted to a bit of inter-Service one-upmanship, but C-in-C Eastern Naval Command did co-operate and order air-strikes on Chittagong and Cox's Bazar, even though the Fleet was better poised for a strike on Barisal where enemy troop concentrations were reported. Such decisions in war underline the need for a theatre Commander. Mountbatten, a young Rear Admiral when being appointed to Burma in 1943 insisted on being designated Supreme Allied Commander. He said, "In an efficient planning organization on high level; there should be no doubt who is in Command of the whole show." He felt that if he was to fulfil his duties, it was essential that some organization should be evolved which would allow him to inject his own ideas at every stage into all plans, including executive plans, before any degree of finality had been reached. No wonder when the Quebec Conference ended, the Combined Allied Chiefs of Staff agreed to give full powers to the recently promoted Admiral Mountbatten and designated him Supreme Allied Commander with overriding powers. In this case, however, the request was from Dewan though not an order was complied by Krishnan. Another example of inter-Service cooperation.

The Defence Minister, Jagjivan Ram was given ocular proof of the sinking of INS Ghazi and on 9 December he announced the Eastern Fleet achievement, which had taken place off Vizag on 3/4 December. The news was received in Parliament with great ovation.

Despite the orders to attack Cox's Bazar and Chittagong, efforts on Barisal were also kept up. Alizes went into the area with moonlight conditions but no movement of ships was observed in Tetuha, Bighai and Bisukali rivers in the Barisal area. The 'Tigers' were luckier and in their second wave of six Seahawks in the Barisal, Bakarganj and Patuawali areas they located and destroyed three enemy barges laden with troops, arms and equipment, in addition to attacking Pakistani troop concentrations and gun positions. This again proved Krishnan's view to decimate troop concentrations in preference to airfields.

The hard-pressed Pakistani troops looked to escape by any means. All riverine craft were pressed into service and merchant ships well disguised in order to obtain permit to save themselves.

These were the targets the IAF and Naval Aerial Forces then addressed themselves to.

Pakistani ships began a ruse to assume neutral colours and Baquir was intercepted.

Early hours of 9 December saw the Eastern Fleet intercepting enemy merchant ships. Four Pakistani tugs were intercepted along with the merchant ship Baquir tried the trick of flying a UN flag and painting a big caption—"UN Supplies for Humanitarian Relief"—on her sides. But the Indian fleet could not be tricked. The ship carried on board contraband and had 4 Pakistani officers and 18 soldiers. Some tugs tried to escape but 4.5" gun fired across their bows was enough to line them up towards Indian ports.

The interception of a merchant ship which was named Azul Hasan Maru near the entrance to the Pusur river proved to be the most dramatic. The ship, was actually Anwar Baksh, a 7,235-ton Pakistan merchant ship and carried hundreds of six foot tall Pathans posing as labourers, who were in fact seasoned soldiers. A boarding party of 18 under Lt Cdr Raz Bazaz of INS Beas boarded the ship. When he discovered the ship's actual crew, he relayed that his 18-man boarding party was too small to physically contain such a large number of soldiers. He then got a report that a sentry had to shoot a Pakistani jawan who tried to attack him. Armed with a light machine gun, Raz Bazaz went forward and there found the mob in a frenzy ready to attack. He warned them to be silent and behave, when they threatened him. He fired a shot in the air but seeing the leader of the mob lead an assault, he opened up rapid fire and just two feet from him the leader fell in a pool of blood. Courage and timely action brought to Sandheads and all crew taken prisoner: Raz Bazaz was an unsung hero, a modest man who, upset and depressed by the incident kept a low profile and hence failed to be even mentioned in dispatches. Hindsight is great sight and large mouths did comment that he should have avoided the killings. Raz Bazaz has since left the Navy.

In the West

Whilst the Fleet was still to flex its muscles, the second raid on Karachi was let loose. INS Trishul (F 15 Captain K.M.V. Nair) and INS Talwar (Cdr. S.S. Kumar) were ordered to rendezvous the missile boat INS Vinash (Lt Cdr Vijay Jerath) and proceed for a strike on Karachi. The media reports are telling and the mood may be summed up in a poem thus:

ONWARDS TO KARACHI

Now take courage my lads, Tis to Karachi we steer
To add something more to this wonderful 1971 year
Tis to honour I call you, as free Indians, not slaves
For who are so free as the sons of Bharat's waves.

Come cheer up my lads, Tis to Karachi we steer
The prize clearer than all, the Indian's dear,
To honour your country, and your Navy,
Be always ready sailorman and stand steady.

Come load up my lads, Tis to targets we steer
Missiles we'll fire, build on the crest of none we fear
And again and repair to Karachi my hands
And yet return to mother and our beloved land.

—The Song of the Missile Boats, 1971

How the Media Saw It

Banner headlines read: "Indian Navy's finest Hour" "Salute to the Navy, "Navy Does Us Proud Again."

The Times of India Reported:

—Today calls for a salute to the Navy. Vice Admiral Kohli, who heads the Western Fleet, is perfectly entitled to make the claim that the second raid mounted by his men on Karachi harbour is one of the most daring in naval history.

The task force did not confine its attention to Karachi alone. It went as far as Gwadar, a fine harbour 448 km west of Karachi, and to Jiwani, another 48 km away to give them a pounding.

The objective of these raids was probably to show that these faraway places cannot provide a sanctuary to the enemy's hard-pressed fleet.

It may also have been intended to discourage clandestine foreign help to Pakistan. Jiwani is only 24 km on Pakistan's side of its border with Iran.

There are two aspects of the action which call for comment. First, Indian naval units went up to within eight kilometers of Karachi and came back unscathed.

After the sinking of the PNS Khaibar and PNS Shah Jahan the Pakistanis would have been well on their guard, eliminating any possibility of their having been taken by surprise.

But why is it that Pakistan's shore-based aircraft failed to hit back? There is no mention in official briefings here of any raids on Karachi by the IAF during the fateful night. (The IAF did strike, the same night but shunned publicity).

Secondly, the losses that the Pakistan Navy has now suffered would make it impossible to challenge Indian control over the maritime approaches to Pakistan.

On the political front, T.V. Parasuram reported from the United Nations the adoption by the General Assembly of a resolution calling for a halt to the war:

The General Assembly yesterday adopted a pro-Pakistani resolution calling for cease-fire and withdrawal by Indian and Pakistani forces but not for simultaneous settlement of the political issues as the root cause of the crisis.

Indian voting against the resolution said she could never be a party to any resolution which would once again enable the Pakistani Army to resume tits repression in Bangladesh.

Indian Ambassador Samar Sen said Bangladesh had come to stay and no power on earth could undo it.

Pakistan welcomed the resolution—which is merely recommendatory and not mandatory—and pledged co-operation...

The numbers—104 for, 11 against and 10 abstentions—do not tell the whole story. Of the five Permanent Members specially charged under the United Nations Charter with a special responsibility for peace-keeping through the Security Council, only two namely the US and China voted for the resolution introduced by Argentina.

Of the three other Great Powers the Soviet Union voted No and Britain and France abstained.

Meanwhile K.S. Ramaswami reporting in the Times of India (9 December) wrote that the gates of Dacca had opened with the capture of Ashugang, Daudhkhandi and Chandpur on the eastern bank of the Meghna river.

Other reports said:

— PAF is crippled and on defensive, says Air Marshal M.M. Engineer AOC-in-C Western Air Command.
— "Indian naval aircraft today bombed Chittagong airfield and Cox's Bazar and considerably damaged airfield hangars and rail tracks. Fishing craft and small boats on the Karnafauli were seen flying white flags."
— "The Pakistani Army counter-attacked Prigunj in the Rangpur-Dinajpur sector but was beaten back."
— "In the Jessore sector, the whole complex of which Jessore is the focal point is in the hands of the Indian Army.'

A PTI report from Jaipur quoting Southern Command spokesman in Jodhpur said: "Some 2,000 sq. km of Pakistani territories are in Indian hands in Barmer sector. In Rajasthan, Indian troops have continued their advance from Gadra and Khakahrapar and are now in contact with the enemy positions in Nayachor, which is across the border".

"And Now to Dacca" said a front-page headline in the Bombay edition of the Indian express:

With the capture of Comilla, the biggest cantonment in Pakistani-occupied part of Bangladesh, and Brahamanbaria, an important junction to the north of Akhaura, the ring is closing round Dacca whose liberation seems to be nearer at hand than appeared two days ago.

Indian troops fighting with the East Bengal Battalion found Comilla evacuated. The Pakistani troops had abandoned it last night. They are withdrawing without any plan... Their bid is to make for Barisal and Narayanganj from where they hope vainly to effect a get-away.

Fierce fighting raged in the Chhamb Sector where the large concentration of Pakistani troops and tanks launched a massive attack early this morning...

The Indian Air Force, which has been active during the day in contrast to the nocturnal preference of the Pakistani Air Force, today damaged 12 aircraft of the enemy. Indian gunners went for the PAF planes while the

IAF helped blunt the tank attack in the Chhamb Sector. Six tanks were destroyed in today's operation.

10/11 December—The Ninth Day

The Defence Minister announced in Parliament that the Indian armed forces and Mukti Bahini were in full concert with each other. Noakhali was liberated, Jamalpur fell with the surrender of 581 Pak soldiers. Hilli and Mymensingh were liberated and advance to Khulna was on. It was thus that the Padma (Lt Cdr Roy Chaudhry), Palash (Lt Mitter) and Panvel (Lt Cdr J.P.A. Noronha) were in the area to support the Army, to soften up Khulna. Their actions are described in a later chapter.

On the Western front fighting for Kargil and Poonch area was in full swing with a counter-attack in the Chhamb sector. The battles for Nayachor in the Barmer sector and capture of Chat Bhet were also going on. As admitted by general Khan in his book, 18 Pak Division had fallen back in Rajasthan by 10 December and the Indian Army regained the initiative by capturing the salient at Islamgarh and three posts.

In the West

The attack on Karachi for the second time was a success and clippings from the Times of India and Indian Express were Salutes to the Indian Navy and speak of the valiant actions of the missile boat commanded by Lt Cdr Vijay Jerath ably assisted by Capt. K.M.V. Nair in the Trishul and Cdr S.S. Kumar in the Talwar. All three officers were awarded Vir Chakras. Whilst the missile boat Captain still serves the Navy, Curly Nair and Kumar left the Navy prematurely for pastures in civil life. They recount the incidents as high-water marks in their professional life. The Fleet was actively engaged in capturing the Madhumati and was still to the south when the sad news of the loss of INS Khukri that went down with 18 officers and 176 sailors off Diu was released. A chapter is dedicated to that loss.

In the Bay

Whilst the ships were fuelled and kept up the pressure the US Naval Task Force consisting of the Enterprises, Decateur and Parsons were on their way into the Bay of Bengal. It would be correct to report that Admiral Zumwalt was not aware of this move and it was leaked by Yeoman Charles Ratford to the Press through his friend Jack Anderson. The Joint Chiefs of Staff head Admiral Tom Moorer who had planned this move by night through the Malacca Straits off Singapore, now found the cat out of the bag. The story has been recounted in Chapter Four in some detail. Once again the Navy looked for specific instructions to deal with the US Task Force. Earlier a Royal Navy Task Force had turned away to Sri Lanka and in the next few days the US Task Force followed suit.

How the Media saw it

— UPI reported Senator Frank Church (Democrat) as remarking that Nixon was seriously considering giving arms to Pindi.

— Reuter reporting from Peking ruled out the possibility of diversionary Chinese moves against India or more concrete backing to Pakistan. Peking would endeavour to show up "Soviet backed Indian aggression" in the world assembly.

— India's air losses heavier for the first time than Pakistan's. Three Air Force planes were lost and one naval plane failed to return.

— Banner headline of 11 December in the Indian Express read "Enemy Thrust in West Halted". In the Western sector in the Chhamb area the Indian Army halted a major attack, the fifth in a row. P.C. Tandon of the Times of India also confirmed this in his report, "Pak Troops Beaten Back in Chhamb".

— With the capture of two gunboats a total of 15 Pakistani vessels are out of action. Merchant ship Baquir was captured. On 9 December Defence Minister Jagjivan Ram made a statement in Parliament in which the sinking of Pakistani submarine Ghazi was confirmed for the first time: … Since my last statement on Tuesday, we have received information that Pakistani's largest submarine, the US built Ghazi was sunk off Visakhapatnam on the night of 3/4 December. When one of our destroyers and a patrol craft were patrolling the approaches of this vital naval base, a submarine contact was picked up. Our ships went into the attack with under-water weapons and a loud explosion followed. The next morning while naval authorities were investigating the area with the help of local fishermen, one of them picked up a life jacket. Bad weather and preoccupation with operations in the Bay of Bengal hampered investigations. Conclusive evidence was obtained only yesterday when three bodies were picked up. These have been identified as Pakistani sailors.

"From the papers obtained from the bodies, it was clearly established that the sunken ship is the Pakistani submarine Ghazi. There are no survivors. The three bodies were accorded a naval burial at sea yesterday."

Swaminathan S. Aiyar of the Times of India summed up the action of 10 December as follows:

In Bangladesh, Indian troops today put themselves in a position to launch a final assault on Dacca by crossing the Meghna river at Ashuganj.

Apart from crossing Meghna, Indian troops occupied the river ports of Mongla and Chalna in Khulna district headquarters was freed by the Mukti Bahini.

In the Jessore sector, Indian troops are fighting on the outskirts of Lalmonihar Ghat, a vital town on the Madhumati River, that guards the route to Faridpur and Goalundo Ghat. Phulpur, 22 km west of Mymensingh has been freed.

The tally of losses as seen by the Indian Express was, Pakistan aircraft 75, tanks 129, warships 3, submarines 2, gunboats 12, India aircraft 33, tanks 49.

A Pakistani vessel masquerading as a Japanese ship was captured with about 500 Pakistani military personnel on board. More than 100 barges and small boats being used by Pakistani soldiers in Bangladesh rivers had been sunk by the IAF.

The next day S. Dharmarajan reported from Calcutta in the Liberation forces of the Indian Army in their multi-pronged thrust towards Dacca, had by this evening cleared the area east of the Meghna of the enemy and also blasted their way into Hilli, Mymensingh and the garrison town of Jamalpur

Hilli, right on the border with West Bengal, which had witnessed ding-dong battle for over a week, was liberated this noon.

About the same time Mymensingh and Jamalpur fell to Indian soldiers marching from the northeast. The capture of Mymensingh paves the way for a strong south-ward thrust towards Dacca...

The retreating forces of the Pakistani army, meanwhile, have blown up the famed Hardinge rail bridge over the Padma near Parbatipur, close to Rajshahi.

12/13 December—The Eleventh Day

In the Comilla sector 1000 Pak troops surrendered, whilst some were attempting escape into Burma. It was evident that the noose on the Pak troops was tightening. On 12 December Indian para-troops were dropped in sizable strength to mount an assault on Dacca, which was gripped by panic. The prisoner of war (POW) camps were expanding fast as surrendering troops, now over 3,000, gave up their arms. The rough tally as it stood for the last ten days of the war, as reported by media, is given below and has been corroborated with the Times weekly report. On this day, however, IAF suffered major losses in the air.

Losses	Pakistan (Total)	East	India (Total)	East
Aircraft	80	20	39	5
Tank	148	0	54	0
Warship	3	0	1	0
Submarine	0	1	0	0
Gunboats/Minesweepers	16	14	0	0

On 13 December General Manekshaw in his third successive message to Gen. Farman Ali re-emphasized the need to surrender and offered just treatment for the troops to avoid shedding of innocent blood. President Nixon also seemed concerned about the war and discussions in the National Security Council mooting means to end the war were discussed seriously. Mrs. Gandhi spoke at the Ramlila grounds in Delhi. Without naming any country she hinted at USA's desire to fight communism and stand for liberty, and yet elaborated how the same country made overtures to China and sided with Pakistan in military pacts. She also hinted at the subjugation of East Pakistan's voice of independence. Maj. Gen. Farman Ali appealed to the UN Secretary-General U Thant for help in repatriating his troops home, which Gen. Yahya Khan asked U Thant to disregard. The morale of the Pak forces in the East was at low ebb. News of five Pak civilian planes landing in Akyab, Burma to evacuate personnel also appeared in the Press. On the Western sector, was a comparative stalemate but aerial activity was noticed off Baroda and Jamnagar. Fighting continued in the Kargil sector and the recapture of three posts there led to restoration of communications to Leh. The Dera Baba Nanak and Poonch sectors there saw sporadic firing and reports indicated that the enemy were forming up for an attack in the Pathankot-Samba sector, five kilometers south of Sohjra. In the Chhamb sector, where Indian troops had scored a victory, it was quiet. In the Jaipur area the Indian troops were carrying out mopping-up operations, after the battle for Nayachor.

In the Bay

The period 11th to 14th was perhaps the most crucial of the war to ensure a total blockade by the Indian Navy which led to an early surrender. Intelligence of Pakistan's last-ditch stance taken in the East was indicated by the information that:

Two coasters ready at Gupta crossing. A/A defences strengthened and runway repaired. All foreign ships cleared off the harbour. Own [Pak] five merchant ships disguised. Naval personnel deployed in defensive position and integrated with fortress defence. Further mining of approaches will be carried out.

This meant that the Pakistan Navy which had acquired British and Chinese mines was being readied for defensive mining, and for disrupting the port of Chittagong. It was tantamounting to a last-ditch action by the Pakistani naval authorities in the East.

The C-in-C East, Krishnan understood the situation and apprised in a signal to the Fleet that senior officer of the enemy were planning to escape to Burma by air or by hugging the coast. Approaches to harbour were likely to be mined. Your mission, he said, is

—To put Chittagong airport out of commission;
—Attack ships both by air and surface units in harbour if they break out.
—This is probably the most important mission of the war in the East. The enemy must be destroyed.
Good Luck.

In response, the aircraft from the Vikrant pounded Chittagong, Barisal and Rajapur. The Cherinpa airfield 32 km north of Cox's Bazar was subjected to air attack and possibly the ground fire was minimal. Ships of the fleet now closed in for bombardment. This exercise called Naval Gunfire support practiced on islands like Pigeon near Karwar and Batti Malv off Andamans became a reality.

In response to the C-in-C's call, a ferocious attack was mounted by the Eastern Fleet throughout 11 and 12 December. Sortie after sortie was flown. The pilots took incredible risks to execute the mission against very surprisingly heavy anti-craft fire. They had been brought in by way of mobile batteries.

Ships of the Eastern Fleet closed in for bombardment taking a calculated risk against the mines reported to have been laid by the enemy. Reporting on this bombardment, one the ships has this to say:

The most conspicuous landmark, the twin casuarinas was visible now. Soon the white buildings in the backdrop of a low dark hill came into vision. Barely five miles off the town of Cox's Bazar, in broad daylight—it was a most daring attack. The colour of water turned into a muddy brown as ships crossed the 10 fathom line. The course was altered to port to bombardment course 340 degrees. Yes, the flag atop the air-traffic control tower was now visible. "All Positions, this is GDP—we will carry out a direct bombardment", flashed the orders. A young sailor was seen caressing every shell. For him the time had come to settle an old score. A few years back his parents were compelled to leave their home in Dacca due to atrocities committed by the military rulers of Pakistan. He was only an infant then. Now, as he stood at his place of duty, he wondered if any of the members of his family left in the then East Pakistan were still alive.

But his ears, like everybody else's on board, were trained for the three words of order, "Four, five, engage."

The guns belched flame, the first salvos leaving the barrels found their mark and the control tower was hit.

Down correction was applied, and instead of the usual Sabre jets the runway received the strange birds, 4.5" shells lading on it. "Left Correction", and a hangar was all in flames. "Right correction", and this time the targets were the enemy barracks. The pause between the corrections witnessed the utter confusion in the enemy—vehicles moving in all directions and men running helter-skelter fleeing for their lives.

The real effect of the shelling was known only when the Mukti Bahini and the local people met our sailors a few days later. It was in this meeting that the Captain of the Beas was informed that an officer named Miya Qasim of Pakistan Air Force was holding a conference when the tower was bombarded. Miya Qasim was killed on the spot along with many of his colleagues. It came to light that this officer had perpetrated the most inhuman atrocities on the local population and was one of the most notorious Pakistani military tyrants in Bangladesh. The jubilation on his death may well be imagined.

Freedom fighters of the Mukti Bahini also disclosed later that seeing the warships so close to the town the enemy became panicky and thinking that landing of troops was imminent ran for dear life. The whole or a garrison left for Burma in a convoy of trucks; and the liberated town fell into the hands of freedom fighters.

Observers later identified the following ships as wrecks in Chittagong, Khulna, Chalna, Mongla and Pussur river.

Pakistani naval ships—Town Class, 6 patrol boats; 3 out of 4 gunboats of the Rajshhai class namely, PNS Jessore, Comilla, Sylhet; at least 6 other gunboats surrendered:

Pak merchant ships damaged included Karnaphuli (6876 GRT); Surma (5890 GRT); Al Abbas (9142 GRT); Anis Baksh (6273 GRT);.

Only PNS Rajshhai under Command of Lt Sikandar Hayat escaped.

As the Media Saw It

The Indian Express special correspondent Binoy Gupta reported the "Battel of Dacca" from Calcutta:

'The 'Operation Bangladesh' reached its climax when the battle for Dacca began today. Indian troops have also launched an attack on Daulatpur cantonment in Khulna.

The troops and naval personnel are also closing in on the port of Chittagong.

An 'adequate force' was air-dropped in an around Dacca both yesterday and today...

Some of the foreigners who were evacuated from Dacca said the people were cheering and clapping as the Indian Air Force bombed he military targets and air-dropped troops.

The Mukti Bahini was also engaged in fierce fighting with the enemy in the area. About 2,000 guerrillas were operating in the city.

With the capture of Narsingdi, the main column that was advancing on land route from Bhairab Bazar had advanced within 25 miles of Dacca.

Two other columns were also advancing by river routes from Chandpur and Daudkandi in the Comilla Sector...

While prisoners have also been taken in the mopping up operations in Laksham and Chandpur, there came the revelation that enemy troops had begun to get into their naval craft to escape. The units of the Indian Navy, which have been busy in this region, intercepted a number of them and sent them down to the bottom of the Bay of Bengal...

Among the areas liberated today were Pheramara, on the southern side of the Hardinge Bridge, and the police stations of Khaksha and Kumarkhali. The Kuthi-bari post of Rabindranath Tagore at Silaidaha and the ancestral house of the great revolutionary, Jatindra Nath Mookerjee, are situated in the liberated areas.

The naval aircraft of the Eastern Fleet continued to strike against Chittagong.

The Indian warships under the direction of naval aircraft engaged and sank six naval craft which were trying go get away. Five others were damaged.

Naval aircraft carried out reconnaissance of the Maskashal river in Cox's Bazar area in Bangladesh and destroyed one gunboat. Two other vessels were damaged.

The carrier-based aircraft carried out bombing raids at Rajapur and near Barisal, damaging military installations in the area yesterday morning.

Cheringa air strip, 32 km north of Cox's Bazar, was also attacked yesterday morning. The runway was damaged.

India suffered the first loss of a frigate in the Arabian Sea. Details were not made available for operational reasons.

A PTI report carried on 13 December said:

Naval aircraft from the aircraft carrier INS Vikrant are creating havoc, confusion and panic with every sortie in the coastal towns of Bangladesh where the Pakistani military machine is still holding out.

A naval observer reported that on Saturday (11 December), a ship of about 1,000 tons drifted into the Bay of Bengal without a single person on board. The vessel had been abandoned in such a hurry that one of two life boats was seen dangling loosely from its rope falls and crashing against the ship's side.

The Indian Navy holds sway over the Arabian Sea and the Bay of Bengal.

Pakistan has confirmed that it is the Indian Navy which rules the waves off its coast. In a merchant broadcast it has warned all merchant shipping that they would approach Karachi at their own risk.

Pakistan has tried to make it appear that it is issuing the warning of its own volition. Observers feel that it has no option but to recognize the fact.

The Indian naval authorities had decided to warn neutral ships off the area of conflict following the damage to a British ship. The Union Government has expressed regret over this.

Midway through the war Inder Malhotra wrote a leader article in the Times of India on "The Indian Navy's Finest Hour—The Triumph and After":

...as far as free India's own sea power is concerned, it is the first time that Indian warships have gone into action since Admiral Kanoji Angre f the Marathas and the Zamorin of Calicut unsuccessfully challenged the naval might of the British who were able to conquer this country at least partly because of the sad neglect of the sea by the Moghuls.

A frontal attack on Karachi, the pride and the main base of the enemy navy, would by itself have been a remarkable achievement. To bag three enemy warships in a single engagement, barely 20 miles from the Pakistani shore, without any loss to our naval task force, makes the achievement sensational. But what makes it altogether unique in maritime history is that the performance was repeated within 72 hours with such audacity as to send the Indian fleet within eight miles of the shore batteries at Karachi and to attack the entire 300-mile Pakistan coast from there to Gwadar to Jiwani.

The Eastern Fleet has, in the meantime, established its supremacy in the Bay of Bengal. It has not only blockaded the West Pakistani-occupied Bangladesh ports completely but also relieved the Air Force of the task of bombing enemy targets in the riverine delta in Bangladesh to enable it to attend to more urgent tasks elsewhere...

This has been the result of the wise decisions of the Naval Headquarters to assign the aircraft-carrier, Vikrant, to the Eastern Fleet although the Western Fleet which had it for years was naturally sorry to let it go.

The details of the brilliant naval actions so far are better known than the broad strategy behind them or the causes of its success. It is now clear that the Naval Headquarters decided to go in for a strategy of bold and daring action based on an intelligent anticipation of, or accurate intelligence about, the enemy's intentions.

Out admirals had rightly calculated that, as in the air, so on the sea, the Pakistanis would attempt a pre-emptive strike. Nothing could confirm this assessment more clearly than the presence of Pakistan's submarine—the American-built Ghazi—off Visakhapatnam at exactly the same time when the PAF planes were attacking Indian air bases on the evening of December 3. But the Indian warships not only sent the Ghazi to the bottom of the sea but also took other counter-measures...

Having thus foiled Pakistani designs, the Indian Navy put into operation the second part of its strategy of attacking the enemy in its citadel, with result which are already well known...

This is not all. Since the beginning of the Indian naval attacks, Pakistan's foreign trade has been almost completely immobilized. On the other hand, the Indian merchant ships, temporarily confined to the ports at the start of hostilities, are once again on the high seas...

But this does not mean that the Pakistani Navy is in no position to act at all. No war can be wholly one-sided as is shown by the loss of an old frigate through Pakistani submarine action. However, when all is said and done there can be no doubt about the supremacy of the Indian Navy in both East and West.

An intriguing feature of Pakistan's pathetic performance on the sea has been the utter failure of its Air Force to come to the aid of its Navy even at Karachi. One reason for this has been the almost perfect co-ordination between the Indian Navy and the Indian Air Force...

In directing the co-ordinated war effort of the three sister Services, the Indian High Command is not unaware of recent history. It knows that the almost complete victory of the Chinese and North Korean forces during the Korean war was undone by the Inchon landings of the US troops...

Sooner or later—sooner rather than later—the liberation of Bangladesh will be complete, and in this the Indian Navy will have played its part with distinction.

15 December—The Thirteenth Day

The end was approaching. Lt Gen. Raina of 2 Corps was mopping up the Jessore Sector. Lt Gen. Sagat Singh of 4 Corps ruled over the Sylhet upto Meghna whilst Maj. Gen. Dalbir Singh 9 Division had approached Khulna in strength. Brig. Hardev Singh Kher with 95 Brigade had already paradropped 500 troops at Tangrail 61 miles north of Dacca and was to capture Lt Col Sultan Ahmed of the 31 Baluch. This was possible because the Mukti Bahini provided full support.

In the Western sector, Lt Gen. Tikka Khan was being restrained in the Chhamb sector and Lt Gen. K.P. Candeth in Sialkot sector had gained his ground. In the Rajastahn and Barmer Sector ably commanded by Lt Gen. G.C. Bewoor the Army had occupied 3000 sq. miles of Pak territory.

In the Bay

To encircle the retreating Pakistani forces, the Indian Navy had planned an amphibious landing south of Cox's Bazar. One battalion of Gurkhas was embarked in the Vishwa Vijaya of the Shipping Corporation of India and the Gharial (Lt Cdr A.K. Sharma) and Guldar (Lt Cdr U. Dabir). The amphibious force under Commander Vernon Rebello proceeded for the operation. Initially the deep water gap between the beach and the ships created a setback with the death of two jawans. Yet under the difficult circumstances boats were commandeered by the Navy and a landing was completed to allow the encirclement to progress. It was an operation conducted in the heat of the war and the full narrative of this will one day be made public. It was Indian Navy's Navy Day—15 December—and as ENC News puts it:

The landing force was sailed from Calcutta on 12 December. Preliminary phase reconnaissance was carried out by Alize and a spot was selected. The beach was bombed on 14 December. The frogmen did a good job investigating the beach head. The LSTs arrived at their destination late in the night of 15th as planned earlier. Everything was going fine. One of the LSTs was beached and the first wave landed. More platoons in successive waves followed. Cox's Bazar was in our hands and the southern route was firmly and finally cut off. Pakistan's trapped soldiers had the alternative of death or surrender.

In the West

The Western Fleet was basking in the glory that it was intact, the blockade was complete and MV Madhumati, a Pakistani merchant ship had been captured. News reports showed that the Captain of the Madhumati, who had earlier served in India, was very much at home. He was interrogated and gave intelligence that the Pakistani Naval Fleet was ailing and had remained in the vicinity of Karachi. No wonder the Indian Fleet did not come to battle.

The next day, the 14th day of the war, was the day of the surrender.

As the Media Saw It

"Dacca Army Chief Seeks Truce", said the banner headline in the Times of India on 15 December, with the story that ran:

Lt Gen A.A.K. Niazi, the West Pakistani occupation Army Chief in Bangladesh who had boasted he would fight to the last man and not surrender, today informed the Chief of the Army Staff, Gen. S.H.F.J. Manekshaw, that he was willing to stop fighting and sought facilities for the repatriation of his forces to West Pakistan abroad vessels of the U.S. Seventh Fleet, diplomatic sources said.

The sources said Gen Niazi's move was a variation of the abortive proposal made last week by another top Pakistani Army official in Bangladesh, Maj Gen Rao Farman Ali, who had sought United Nations assistance for the repatriation of the beleaguered occupation forces. Significantly Gen. Niazi's communication bore Gen Farman Ali's signature as a witness.

As a token of good faith, Gen Manekshaw directed the cessation of air action over Dacca, where Gen. Niazi and his forces were holding out.

The Indian troops were holding the city in a tight ring at the time of these dramatic developments. The many columns that had advanced to the city from different directions were only two kilometers away.

The Voice of America, quoting a report from Dacca, said...that President Yahya Khan had, in a message to Gen. Niazi advised him to stop fighting if necessary.

"Pak Troops Give up in Desh" was the headline in the Times of India the next day:

Bangladesh was freed today from the colonialist yoke of West Pakistan when its occupation forces under the command of Gen Niazi surrendered to the combined forces of the Mukti Bahini and the Indian Army.

The instrument of surrender was signed by Lt Gen A.A.K. Niazi, Chief of the Pakistani Army in Bangladesh, at 4.31 p.m. IST and was accepted by Lt Gen Jagjit Singh Aurora, General Officer C-in-C, Eastern Command.

Radio Pakistan, while making no mention of the surrender by the Pakistani forces, told its listeners that the fighting in the Eastern theatre had ended, "following an agreement between the local commanders of India and Pakistan."

THE SINKING OF PNS GHAZI

THE GHAZI LIVES ON

Had the Ghazi lived it would have had a tale to tell
Of hardship, endurance, courage and the tumultuous swell
That would have stirred many a seaman's heart
But alas she fell prey to lack of underwater art.

The remains are rough notes and many a dead body
Found first by Chintapallie of Vizag in a 'todi'
For surely and certainly fourth December seventy one
Was a fateful day when the sea battle began.

The Ghazi instead of stalking the Vikrant
Exploded not far from Vizag's sea front
For the Indian Navy it was a lucky shot
On what was the very first day of the victory trot.

The proud countrymen of Pakistan did learn
Of the sad loss on the very same morn
That they bore the wrath of missiles on Karachi Fort.
Set forth by the brave killers who went for that very port.
Now only a memory of those ninety lives
And many who depended on them and their wives
Live by the meaning of what was the Ghazi.
For defender of that faith is the new PNS Ghazi.

Luck favours the brave. Service leaders often quote this saying in their war briefing. Napoleon is said to have always chosen the general who he thought was lucky for a mission from amongst those names which were put before him. In war, as in love, an element of chance always exists and so discussion will go on, whether it was Pakistan's ill-luck or a deliberate attack that sent PNS Ghazi (Cdr Zafer Mohammed Khan) to a watery grave few miles off Visakhapatnam on the night of 3-4 December 1971, with no survivors at all. Was it that they were not brave, or was it that INS Rajput and another patrol craft Akshay, which were both on patrol off Visakhapatnam, scared them with a depth-charge attack to dive deep and hit the bottom of the sea? Did a mine explode in the submarine's vulnerable hull when attempting to lay mines? Did the submarine suffer some mechanical problem and lose buoyancy and dive into Davy Jones Lockers? (Originated from 'Divya Loka' the Hindu God of the Sea and Anglicized to become Davy Jones Locker.) All these are moot questions and can never be answered with certainly for not one of those 90 on board is left to tell the true tale. Yet it is true that the Indian Navy's luck was very much the contributive cause for the Ghazi's demise, just when the war had begun— and it was luck too that aided the brave Indian Navy.

PNS Ghazi was formerly USS Diablo, a Tench-class submarine built at the US naval shipyard at Portsmouth. It was given on lease for training of Pakistan Navy personnel as part of the US military aid programme. The Pakistan Navy as it were, entered the submarine era earlier than the Indian Navy by acquiring this submarine on 1 June 1964. Till then only a handful of Indian officers and sailors had been t rained in UK at HMS Dolphin in Portsmouth under the UK Military Training Assistance Programme (UKMTAS) and were to form the nucleus of the Indian Navy's submarine arm when eventually four F class submarines (Kalvari, Khanderi, Karanj and Kursura) were acquired progressively from the Soviet Union in 1968-70. The Ghazi was comparatively old boat in 1971 but had long-range capability and had thus been deployed on patrol 1,500 miles away from Karachi presumably to attack the Vikrant which, Admiral Krishnan, by a ruse, had promulgated would be off Visakhapatnam. The Submarine must have been stealthily waiting for this prey. Even though a clause existed in the US-Pakistan loan deal that the Ghazi would be used only for training purposes, one reckons that such an agreement goes overboard in a real-time threat situation.

The events leading to the announcement of the sinking of the Ghazi as reported in a leading newspaper makes interesting reading.

SINKING OF GHAZI

Express New Service

10 Dec.—The Pakistani attempt to sink the biggest prize of all—INS Vikrant, India's aircraft carrier—was nullified by the Eastern Naval Command on December 3 by sinking its submarine Ghazi. The fact that the submarine was so close to Visakhapatnam within seven hours of Pakistan's treacherous air attack on Indian on the evening of 3 December tells its own tale.

This is positive proof of the pre-planned aggression by Pakistan against India, says Vice-Admiral N. Krishnan, Flag Officer Commanding-in-Chief of Eastern Naval Command.

On obtaining a contact, an urgent attack was carried out with depth charges. But they did not find any sound. They alerted fishermen going into the sea to look out for anything floating.

Chintapalli Satyalu and Chintapalli Achayya of Kotha Jalaripeta here found a life jacket floating near Visakhapatnam.

Next day, Naval personnel went with them and found it at the same spot.

Both the fishermen were awarded Rs. 500 each. The district Collector has also been requested to reward them.

Vice-Admiral Krishnan described the story of the end of the Pakistani submarine as follows:

"On the night of the third, after the treacherous attack by Pakistan, it was appreciated that a pre-emptive underwater attack against the Naval Base at Visakhapatnam might be imminent and local naval defences were immediately put in readiness.

In addition to all precautions within the harbour, two ships sailed out just before midnight on a mission.

On obtaining a contact, an urgent attack was carried out with depth charges. The south was, however, lost after the attack and the ship proceeded on her mission to join other units out at sea.

Shortly after midnight and just before the Prime Minister's broadcast to the nation, a very loud explosion was heard rattling several window panes in buildings near the beach.

This was reported to me by our coast battery which was awaiting any likely surface attack on Visakhapatnam.

We assumed that the explosion heard was probably the result of our attack and commenced our searches. The Eastern Naval Command Headquarters, as part of defence preparedness, had enlisted the support of all local fisher-folk and they had been thoroughly briefed on what to do in events such as these.

According to these instructions while the search was on, two fishermen, on picking up a life jacket and other debris, lost no time in bringing these across to the Command Headquarters.

Further searches could not be very extensive due to bad weather. Yesterday, however, we found three bodies and a lot of flotsam and jetsam. There are ample evidences available from these that the submarine destroyed is none other than the Pakistani ship Ghazi.

In our appreciation of the situation in the event pre-emptive strike by Pakistan, we had always assessed that they would most probably deploy the Ghazi which has a considerable range in the Bay of Bengal and would probably be off Madras or Visakhapatnam and their aim would be sinking the biggest prize of all, the Vikrant.

This appreciation has been proved absolutely correct. The four bodies were given in accordance with Service custom and tradition, a sailor's burial at sea, with proper solemnity and appropriate ceremony.

This submarine Ghazi, which was given to Pakistan by the Americans on 1 June 1964 had been the cause of much worry to our naval planners all these years. And here, at last, she lies at our doorstep as a dead monument and a reminder that aggression does not pay.

The obituary for the Ghazi is: a Tench-class submarine, built by Portsmouth Naval Shipyard, US and transferred to Pakistan Navy, 2410 tons submerged, speed 20 knots on surface and 10 knots submerged, carrying ten 21 torpedoes, six in the bows and four in the stern, radius of action 14,000 miles at 10 knots, complement of 90 officers and sailors."

And the epitaph is a plaque of Urdu couplet found on one of the bodies which says: "We are far from home, when will we see our loved ones again."

The Times of India (7 December) added a footnote: During the 1965 Indo-Pakistan conflict, the Ghazi, meaning 'Defender of the Faith', was damaged by an Indian destroyer. It was sent to Iran for months for repairs and refitting.

The interesting point to note from the Press cuttings is that though the Ghazi sank on the night of 3-4 December the announcement was made to the nation only on 9 December. Eastern Naval Command was the concerned authority and its head was Admiral Krishnan, the clever and extremely brilliant tactician. It appears he did receive news of INS Rajput's depth-charge attack and that of an explosion off Visakhapatnam at about midnight on 3 December, but since no confirmatory news of debris, oil slick or derelict of the submarine were seen or reported by the Rajput, the information was left in the background. It was on the information given by the two fishermen of having sighted a floating life jacket that a search was put into motion. The Nistar, the Indian Navy's diving tender and submarine rescue vessel acquired in the late 1960's from USSR with diving-bell facilities was ordered to get ready to search and go on top of the likely position of the Ghazi for salvage. Thereafter an approximate position of the submarine was established and three floating bodies of Pakistan Navy sailors, brown skinned like Indians, but circumcised, were also located along with some papers, signals, a notice to mariners signed by Pakistan Navy's Chief Hydrographer H. Sawarkhan and a seaman's Knife—all confirmed that the Ghazi lay dead. The Chief of Naval Staff, Admiral Nanda wanted tangible ocular proof and an officer, Lt Cdr Nagrani, a submariner himself, proceeded to Delhi to display these items to their Lordships. These items are now housed in the Maritime Museum at Middle Ground, Bombay. The announcement of the confirmed sinking by the Indian Navy was received by the nation with joy and it brought out further confidence in fleet ships.

Though at that time how the Ghazi sunk remained unclear as it does even today.

The exploits of Pakistan submarines are discussed in this book in various chapters. PNS Hangor was responsible for sinking INS Khukri. The strength of the Pakistan Navy submarine arm in 1971 comprised a total of four submarines, the three 700-ton 'Daphnes', Hangor, Shushak and Mangro, all commissioned in 1970, and the Ghazi was replaced by a new Ghazi in 1975 when the Pakistan Navy purchases the Portuguese Daphne class Cachalote. This means a Ghazi still serves the Pakistan Navy and is a memory to those officers and men who went down on the first day of the war. What was to be the trump card of the Pakistan Navy to stalk the Vikrant and the Eastern Fleet ships, and possibly merchant ships too, entering Visakhapatnam, was foiled. The loss of a submarine must have been realized by the Pakistan Naval Headquarters on 4 December, the night the missile killers attacked and set Karachi ablaze. Can one imagine the plight and the demoralization of that Navy?

The loss of the Ghazi and sinking of the Khukri set this proud arm of the Pakistan Navy thinking soon after the war. The future acquisitions from France were well planned and a separate logistics department was set up. Even today the submarine arm of the Pakistan Navy is elite and has produced two Chiefs of Naval Staff.

INS KHUKRI GOES DOWN

At sea especially in war, the Captain and his team must act unhesitatingly in emergencies which are not infrequent, without orders, in the spirit and manner their common superior would desire.

At sea especially in war, the Captain and his team must act unhesitatingly in emergencies which are not infrequent, without orders, in the spirit and manner their common superior would desire.

The war at sea was going well for Indian and with the first five days bringing their small measures of triumphs—namely the attacks on Karachi, the sinking of the Ghazi and the exploits of the Vikrant; all these had created a tremendous sense of confidence kin this small sea-going arm. The first major blow to the Indian Navy came on the fateful night of 9 December. It rocked the Navy when the reality of actual war hit the sea-going community at large. Whilst the officers and men on board INS Khukri were tuned in to listen to the All India Radio news at 8.50 pm on the ship's SRE (Sound Reproduction Equipment) and were specifically on an anti-submarine warfare mission to look out for a reported Pak submarine, the Khukri was hit by more than one torpedo; possibly three, fired from one of Pakistan Navy's three newly acquired Daphne-class submarines, the Hangor (Cdr A. Tasneem) about 40 miles off Diu Head. In command was Captain Mahendra Nath Mulla a 45-year old tall, strapping royal Navy-trained anti-submarine warfare specialist with earlier command experience of destroyer INS Rana and Second-in-Command of INS Krishna (the Kistna). One can picture him on the bridge of his ship, after helplessly realizing that hope was lost and forced to give the order "Abandon Ship'. The file report from the Times of India of that day is reproduced.

CAPTAIN GOES DOWN AFTER SAVING SHIPMATES

(By a Staff Reporter)

Eighteen officers and 176 sailors went down with the anti-submarine frigate, INS Khukri, as she sank in the Arabian Sea, torpedoed by enemy submarines on the night of Dec 9. Capt. Mahendra Nath Mulla (45) the skipper, stood by his ill-fated shipmates to the last and shared their destiny despite having opportunity to save himself.

The story of the 45-year-old gallant commanding officer's efforts to rescue as many as he could and then going down with his ship was told by eye-witnesses among the survivors now in Bombay.

Many of the younger, inexperienced sailors preferred false security of the sturdy steel deck of the frigate below their feet to the unknown dangers lurking in the bosom of the sea. The 183-cm-tall Captain Mulla himself pushed them into the sea, directing them to swim away. When one of them offered him a life-jacket he said, "Go on, save yourselves: do not worry about me." There was no confusion, no panic because the Captain's calm had transmitted itself to his men.

As the survivors were swimming away to avoid being sucked in by the sinking ship, some of them looked back. The ship was sinking fast and the sea was closing over the bridge, the highest part of the ship's super structure, from where the Captain assumes command. Captain Mulla was sitting in his chair on the bridge.

He had faithfully served to the very last, to the best of his ability, those who had served him so well. Six officers and 61 sailors who have survived will ever remember Captain Mulla's stoic demeanour and calm in the face of adversity. The whole nation will cherish the memory of this hero.

The 1,200-tonne Khukri formed part of the Western Fleet Task Force which was bunting enemy submarines in the Arabian Sea. She was hit by the torpedoes by an enemy submarine at intervals of a few minutes. As soon as Captain Mulla realized that the ship could not be saved, he gave order to the frigate ship's company to abandon the ship.

Then he directed his second-in-command to cast life-boats and buoys into the sea. In carrying out this vital task 33-year-old Lt Commander Joginder Kumar Suri also went down with the ship.

Captain Mulla's story is in the highest traditions. The Captain of ship is the last man to abandon ship when the ship sinks fast, as it often happens in war. Many men are trapped down below and go down with it. A large number of them will be still endeavouring to save the ship as it happened in the case of the Khukri.

"While the highest traditions of a Captain going down with his are fully appreciated, the Royal Navy cannot afford to lose experienced commanding officers. They are therefore, to endeavour to save themselves so that they may live to fight another day ..." This was the British Admiralty Order during World War II. It might well be so, but Captain Mulla followed the traditions set for captains of going down with the ship when all endeavours to save it proved futile. Captain Mulla was awarded MVC posthumously.

The sinking has evinced very keen discussion on the issues that such large casualties, resulting in loss of life of this nature, throw up. Was Indian Navy's damage control ability in doubt? Can two or three torpedoes of L-60 variety sink a ship like the Khukri specially built for anti-submarine warfare with British 170/174 sonar sets and Mortar MK 10? What speed was the ship doing? What after-accident search and rescue measures were taken to reduce loss of life? The discussion still goes on, but some factors are touched upon in this chapter along with some facets of human life.

The Khukri was well manned, worked up, and the Second-in-Command of the ship Lt Cdr J.K. Suri, 33, a bachelor, was in fact, a specialist communications officer. An excellent Navy squash player, unfortunately he was a poor swimmer. He was on the bridge when the torpedoes hit. The story has it that because the ship lost power and went down in minutes, some men trying to get out of the ship in darkness from below deck ran into those like J.K. Suri going down to fetch their life jackets. The Khukri had only two exits and over 100 men crowding these two exit ports must have caused panic and in the melee they would have got crushed whilst the ship went down. Yet the Captain helped each one he could see on the bridge to leave the ship. Commander Oomen, the tough and plump Malayali Engineer Officer may have decided to go down to the Engine Room like so many other dedicated sailors who are trained, by instinct, to rush to their action post-and suffered a watery death. Lt Suresh Kundanmal, a fine 'Sword of honour' officer is reported to have jumped over the side after coaxing his Captain to do so too, but could have well got sucked into the whirlpool caused by the sinking ship.

All this is reported by survivors like Lt Manu Sharma, another fine officer who has since left the Navy and settled in USA. He was extremely shaken when rescued back to Bombay, borrowing clothes and uniforms like all the others and cautioned not to talk to anyone. All such happenings leave scars on people and so it was for the rescued survivors of the Khukri. It was a shocked Navy trying to cope with an unprecedented situation. Whilst surviving officers and men wanted to talk, take things off their chest, and seek reassurance from the silent and awaited the inquiry that followed. After all, war-fare at sea has proved that the submarine with its stealth is still superior and can only be killed after it has killed and shown herself.

The successful attack by a Pakistan Navy submarine was possible because it is commonly known that INS Khukri was doing only 12 knots. Lt V.K. Jain, a bright Electrical Officer, who has researched on an attachment to improve the sonar performance of the 170/174 set was, unfortunately, testing his hardware on board. It is known that Captain Mulla did not favour this slow speed but he had to give into this young officer's request. One of those misfortunes, combined with the fact this class of ship did not have a strong shipside and thus succumbed to damage easily. It is also possible that the Pakistan Navy submarine had tracked the Khukri for some time by keeping in company with some fishing craft which were earlier in the vicinity. The officers and crew were possibly not at their best alert whilst concentrating on the news bulletin, even though the ship's company was at defence stations. The crews were also not wearing life jackets continuously because even in World War II this practice was not followed. (The story of the "Kappkkid", a navigator who kept his Kapok life jacket on at all times and was lone survivor in World War I, Murmansk Convoy is famous. He did it even though he was ridiculed. Modern warfare may not allow time to fetch one.)

INS Kirpan (Cdr R..R.. Sood) was in company and that ship also did not gain any submarine contact. This then was the fate of INS Khukri. The hit caused the few on upper deck, to be thrown out into the sea. The ship's Physical Training Instructor (PTI) held on to a piece of wood the whole night. Some took to life rafts, some lay in their life jackets awaiting rescue.

A major decision lay on the broad shoulders of the Captain of INS Kirpan, Cdr R..R.. Sood (awarded the Vir Chakra and now Rear Admiral). Should he pick up survivors, hunt the submarine or clear the area? He decided to clear the area, signaled the happenings as a witness and requested the Flag Officer commanding-in-Chief, Western Naval Command, Bombay for help. In the operation that followed INS Kadmatt (Cdr S. Jain, now Flag Officer commanding in chief Western Naval command) and Kripan arrived at the scene the next morning and carried out rescue operations. A total of eight officers and 61 men were rescued, whilst 18 officers and 176 sailors went down. A memorial was erected for them on the coast near Diu, and every time a thoughtful Captain sails past the position where the Khukri memorial hostel was built at Bombay to house the widows and fatherless children of the ill-fated ship. A few days later, the parents of Lt V.K. Jain instituted the Jain memorial medal for excellence in innovation. Till another Khukri is commissioned, their memory will live on.

The reaction on the other ships in the fleet was naturally one of sadness. But it also acted as a warning. Anti-submarine warfare drills improved, torpedo evasion technique was practiced earnestly, life jackets and life raft release inspections and drills were exercised meticulously. Ships began to see themselves in a similar situation and attended to their damage control arrangements. It cannot be said that it was an expensive blessing in disguise, bit it can be said that this event certainly did make its point, the Indian Navy now realizing what submarine torpedo attacks are all about.

While the Pakistan Navy achieved a kill through the sinking of the Khukri, the three Indian Navy submarines of the F class deployed on offensive patrols failed to achieve any kills. The restrictions on submarines are many. They were banned by law to sink merchant ships. The London Naval Arms Limitation Treaty of 1930 declared that submarines "may not sink or render incapable of navigation a merchant vessel without having first placed passengers, crew and ships papers in place of safety". The Indian Navy was in the same dilemma in 1971 and had restricted its submarines to firing only on enemy warships that were positively identified. Since the chance of being sunk itself by a warship if she exposed herself, were high, it amounted to prohibition in a larger sense and inhibiting the freedom of a submarine commander in war.

The period after the war was traumatic for the families of those reported missing. Lt. Suresh Kundanmal's family got reports that many survivors had drifted away and that Suresh had been able to swim to safety after having given his life jacket to another. Astrologers too, assured the family that he was alive. Hope lived on for many. J.K. Suri's brother at the Ashoka Hotel did not settle the family assets hoping his bachelor brother would return. Meanwhile, a polite message went out to all Captains at sea which ordered them not to emulate Captain Mulla's traditional Captain-go-down-with-his ship attitude; but to save the experience to fight another day.

A few weeks after the war some fine sailors from the Khukri joined INS Nilgiri, India's first Leander, as part of rehabilitation of the crew. The Captain of the Nilgiri Captain D.S. Paintal looked upon this act as a superstitious omen, but when assured that they were experienced shipwrecked sailors who could possibly be of help in educating the ship's company of the new Nilgiri, they were welcomed on board warmly like so many others of that ill-fated ship. Incidentally, in the Falklands war, a total of seven warships were sunk, but all their Captains were rescued and live to tell their tale; once again showing off Admiral Nanda's message to his fleet Captains as propitious. One day another Khukri will undoubtedly be commissioned so that we do not forget.

A Nation and its Navy at War

THE KHUKRI IS NO MORE

I am Manu Sharma who served the Navy
Settled now in USA, aged forty-two or thereabouts.

I knew the Khukri which also symbolizes Gurkha strength
And I was on her last voyage wherein served,

Mahendra Nath Mulla the Captain who smoked
His last cigarette as he went down
The old man to the sea.

Thambe Ommen the ship's Engineer who tried his best
But the Arabian Sea engulfed him.

Young Suresh Kundanmal that fine personality
Who gave his life jacket to another,
And lost his life without knowing it.

Joginder Suri who was the executive of the ship
But saw his own execution for he could not swim.

Also down went those smiling one hundred seventy-six Indian Seadogs
The others whose names I remember not
But the Khukri I do.

They all lie some forty miles from Diu
Undisturbed till they are picked up.

And only a wreck marks that special danbuoy stave
Till another Khukri rides India's waves.

Ranjit B. Rai

THE STORY OF ASHOK ROY VRC AND ROY CHOUDHRY VRC

Should auld acquaintance be forgot,
And ne'er brought to mind?
Should auld acquaintance be forgot.
And days o' auld Lang Syne.

Robert Burns.

An unsung hero of the 1971 war is Ashok Roy who served near East Pakistan and later in the Western Sector. A very interesting question of the 1971 war which has not been answered with definite proof is how this fine young pilot Lt Cdr Ashok Roy went down in Alize No. 203 on a flight from Jamnagar to Bombay with Lieutenant Sirohi and Chief Aircrew-man Vijayan. Ashok had endeared himself to each and every one who had come in contact with him. He was an emotional, strapping red-faced officer. Son of Brig A.N. Roy (later Major General) in the Medical Corps of the Army, this well-built six footer was proficient in games, a powerful swimmer and an ace pilot with high grading's. He had done his stint on board INS Vikrant in the Cobra Squadron of Alizes and was transferred to an 'R' class aviators gaining sea experience.

Ashok Roy had been through many scrapes in life. In the late 1960's his eyesight had started to weaken and he prayed to God to heal his eyes so that he could catapult off the deck of the Vikrant again. He had been advised by one and all to pray to God—something he did not normally do. Apparently God heard his prayers, for lo and behold, Ashok was back in AISI medical category and back to the flat-top he loved. In another incident in Cochin, whilst in a car race back from the Sealord Hotel to the naval base Aku was running out of the hotel (giving me a lead in view of my 1946 Juvaquatre Renault as against his 1960 Standard), fell into a ditch and broke his knee. Despite this, he raced all the way to the base, won the race and the prize—only to be admitted in the hospital, plastered and immobilised. He was again advised to pray to God and lay off the girls, and he would be back to his first love—aircraft. Once again Aku recovered fast, got his category and was back to flying.

During the late 1960s the pilots of the Indian Navy were urging their superiors to send them to sea in general service billets to further their naval career prospects. A policy decision was taken and a number of pilots were sent in command and other sea-going billets. Aku landed up in INS Rana as the TAS Officer. He could be seen working on weekends coming to grips with the 144 Q Sonar set.

One day in October 1971, Aku was not there to be seen nor heard of.

Later, one learnt that he had gone off to be with Sammy—Cdr M.N. Samant—and his band operating from Calcutta and presumably engaged in planning on what to do with that huge influx of refugees into West Bengal from East Pakistan. Suddenly, just before the war, an emaciated Aku turned up in Bombay and refused to talk about his exploits. He was pining to go on leave. Just then the war broke out and Aku was back to flying his beloved Alizes, a flying machine that carries good ARAR French electronic equipment, possibly the best at the time. His other colleagues were on the Vikrant in the Eastern Sector and that saddened him a bit.

One next heard of Aku operating from Jamnagar from where the IAF were launching strikes. On a particular day in December during the war, Aku and Alize pilot Lieutenant Dua in another Alize took off from Jamnagar. Aku ordered his junior winger to proceed to Bombay and himself went off to possibly investigate a target given, or on some classified mission. Whatever it was, Aku was never heard of again. He was awarded the Vir Chakra and his citation reads that a Pakistan Air Force plane shot him down. Pakistan Radio did announce shooting down of a plane over the sea, but was Aku there? How, then was he lost? Was he shot down by a Pakistani trawler with anti-aircraft guns? Was he on a secret mission and taken prisoner? If he was shot down, surely Alizes can survive a belly-landing type of ditch, and Aku was a powerful swimmer. Did the Pakistan Air Force actually strafe him to death, a single-engined slow-paced aircraft at that? Was he surprised? Did he suffer engine breakdown? Did he trespass into enemy territory on an early warning mission? Somewhere in the 2500 square miles west of Jamnagar lies the answer to the question of a father in anguish who still enquires.

It is believed that an emissary from Pakistan informed Maj Gen. A.N. Roy that his son was seen with a broken leg in plaster in the Lahore jail along with some East Bengali pilots. When the General tried to arrange his son's escape at some cost to himself, Aku apparently wanted a slight delay. The story goes that Ali was rescued by the Balochi's along with the other pilots and kept in captivity and then in settlement—for he did resemble the Baluchis. This mystery can be solved only by a co-operative answer by the Pak Defence Forces for Sirohi was also not heard of. His wife, Priscilla, left India. Vijayan the aircrew man is the other unsung hero. As time passes, memories also fade. Lest we forget, this chapter is dedicated to them.

Another contemporary human life story is that of Roy Chou who again like Aku, a Bengali officer was whisked away from his gunnery instructor job in Cochin 1971 to work under directions of Capt R.P. Khanna (NOIC Calcutta) and town, Calcutta. His family originally hailed from East Bengal. His aged father had been left behind in East Pakistan when the rest of the family migrated to India during the partition and his family had fallen from Zamindari riches. Roy Chou's brothers sent him to the Prince of Wales

Military College, Dehra Dun. There he excelled in all games and showed his girl. When called up in 1971, he was possibly happy to go to East Bengal even though no immediate family remained there. It was a nostalgic return to his land of birth and he was there for a cause, service to his country, like many others.

During one of his breaks in Calcutta, his wife briefly wrote that Chou seemed to be enjoying his work, but she worried for him after reading the papers. He had left her behind in Calcutta, and there were long stretches when Roy Chou was not heard of. It was his boxing, athletics and football 'Blues' (NDA cadets who achieved high standards) from the National Defence Academy, Khadakwasla, that kept him in fine fettle in whatever he was achieving near enemy lines.

Roy Chou never speaks of what he did, but if asked about the massive shrapnel wound in his leg, the story he tells is interesting: "That I got from the IAF". Apparently by this time he had operated as Captain of a requisitioned fishing craft Padma in concert with the Mukti Bahini and had made forays into Bangladesh. One day during the war a squadron of three boats, under Cdr M.N. Samant in INS Panvel (Lt. Cdr. J.P.A. Noronha, both later decorated MVC), the Padma in concert with the Mukti Bahini and had made forays into Bangladesh. One day during the war a squadron of three boats, under Cdr. M.N. Samant in INS Panvel (Lt Cdr J.P.A Noronha, both later decorated MVC), the Padma and Palash were going up the river to Khulna camouflaged for an attack. They were advised to display a yellow bunting cloth, four feet by four feet square on the ship's bridge top to avoid being strafed by the Indian Air Force and Indian Navy planes. All was well till they neared Khulna in single column, when a formation of our IAF Gnats appeared overhead and began to pull up for a diving run. No one realized the 'snafu', that the yellow bunting was helping the IAF to aim better on otherwise camouflaged boats. When all hell broke loose and their aim meant for the Pakistanis, which was good, was now lashed on Sammy's force, it was Roy Chou saw his boat subjected to another strafing run when he decided to beach his boat and like Capt M.N. Mulla ordered "Abandon ship" when all hope was lost. He was thrown overboard into this tributary of the holy Ganga, and to his good luck INS Panvel sailed inches past him, also manoeuvring in the melee to avoid the friendly Gnats who reappeared. Some of his colleagues shrapnel in his leg and with thoughts of some of his colleagues now no more. He was rescued and hospitalized.

That ended Roy Chou's escapades but it came to light that in the fog of war, instructions like yellow bunting can get fouled up and the message did not reach the IAF Squadron at Kharagpur. Bunting is a typical naval term for cloth woven for naval flags and possibly the story of President John F. Kennedy in World War II came true again. It is said that he always believed in double checking his minor instructions because of a theory he picked up in command of Patrol Boat PT 109, when it ran aground under his command in World War II. He ordered "Abandon ship" and was about to jump overboard assuming that he was the last remaining one on the ship. Just then the phone from his engine room rang and his duty machinist reported, "Captain, I think we are aground". It was then that he coined the phrase, "Some bastard down there may not get the message. Always double-check".

Anyway, Roy Chou was brought back alive to tell the tale of his doings and how he earned his will-deserved Vir Chakra. Regrettably, like many others who toiled and risked their all in war, but possibly did not pick up that good boy's chit called the Annual confidential Report, his name did not appear in the list of those promoted to Commander in 1974. In war, tempers can be frayed. Roy Chou promptly put pen to paper and submitted his resignation, much against the advice John Hopwood gives in Laws of the Navy. When contacted on telephone at Visakhapatnam at the Command Gunnery Office and told to hang on for the next list and withdraw his letter, he replied in a tone which many of his superiors and colleagues had heard as polite, but full of conviction and home truth. "Please tell the Personnel Directorate to Process my papers fast. Some give up their lives for a thing called pride. The least I can do is to give up the service I love for my pride, and what I did in 1971. Do me a favour and get my papers through." Such is what brave mavericks are made of, who fight against odds and lead their men almost in the face of daily death. It is fortunate the Indian Navy was replete with such officers and men in 1971. In peace they are often forgotten, as is the way of the world with soldiers.

THE SURRENDER

It takes more courage to suffer than to die.

—*Napoleon*

With the fate of utter defeat at the hands of the Indian Services; the Indian Army crossing the Meghna on 10 December from Ashuganj; the Indian Air Force ruling the skies and the Indian Navy in complete control of the seas—it was Maj Gen Rao Farman Ali Khan, Military Adviser to the Governor of East Pakistan who took the initiative. He sent a message to U Thant, the UN Secretary-General on 10 December through the UN representative in Dacca proposing a ceasefire, the repatriation of the Pakistani forces to West Pakistan, the evacuation of the Indian force and "A peaceful transfer of power to a government of elected representatives of East Pakistan". President Yahya Khan had previously agreed to this approach, and then countermanded the proposal on 11 December, creating an impasse. The war continued with the Indian advance to Dacca, where the Pakistani command had decided to consolidate.

The evacuation of foreign nationals had commenced on 12 December. And the first sign of surrender came, when on 14 December a Pakistani brigade retreating from Mymensingh surrendered at Tungri, 12 miles north of Dacca. The Commanding Officer was taken prisoner. The count-down had begun.

General Manekshaw now took it upon himself to appeal not to Lt Gen Amin Abdul Abdullah Khan Niazi but to Maj Gen Farman Ali declaring that "Further resistance is senseless and will mean death to many poor soldiers under your command which is quite unnecessary". He promised complete protection and just treatment but General Niazi was adamant to "fight to the last man".

Meanwhile after long discussions with his Ministers, the Governor of East Pakistan, Dr. A.M. Malik, wrote a letter to President Yahya Khan tendering his resignation on the afternoon of 14 December from the air raid shelter in his garden; his official residence had been destroyed in an air raid shortly before. He then took refuge with his family and his Ministers in the Intercontinental Hotel which had been declared a neutral zone for foreigners, wounded soldiers and other non-combatants and was administered by the Red Cross. Sixteen senior officials, including the Inspector-General of Police, had already sought refuge in the hotel.

On 15 December the Indian forces closed in on Dacca from all sides including a para drop. A column advancing from the east crossed the river Lakhya, the last natural obstacle in their way, and began pounding the city with mortars from only a mile or two outside. To the south, troops which had crossed the Meghna from Daudkandi began moving northward. The force which had pursued the retreating Pakistanis from Kushtia succeeded in crossing the Madhumati at Magura, and advanced towards Dacca from the west. At Khulna, where the Pakistanis were still resisting strongly, the Indian Army occupied one of the suburbs.

Since you have indicated your desire to stop fighting, I expect you to issue orders to all forces under your command in Bangladesh to cease fire immediately and surrender to my advancing forces wherever they are located. I give you my solemn assurance that personnel who shall be treated with the dignity and respect, that soldiers are entitled to, and I will abide by the provisions of the Geneva Conventions. Further, as you have many wounded, I shall ensure that they are well cared for and your dead given a proper burial. No one need have any fear for their safety, no matter where they come from, nor shall there be any reprisals by forces operating under my command.

Immediately I receive a positive response from you, I shall direct General Aurora, the Commander of Indian and Bangladesh forces in the Eastern theatre, to refrain from all air and ground action against your forces. As a token of my good faith I have ordered that no air actions shall take place over Dacca from 1700 hours today.

I assure you I have no desire to inflict unnecessary casualties on your troops, as I abhor loss of human lives. Should you, however, not comply with what I have stated, you will leave me with no other alternative but to resume my offensive with the utmost vigour at 0900 Indian Standard Time on 16 Dec.

On the morning of 16 December UN officials in Decca discovered that General Niazi was unable to inform General Manekshaw of his acceptance of these terms because communications at his headquarters had been put out of action by Indian bombing. A message was therefore sent to New Delhi through UN radio facilities, 10 minutes before General Manekshaw's ultimatum was due to expire, requesting for a six-hour extension of the bombing pause and for an Indian staff officer to negotiate the terms of surrender. Maj Gen J.F.R. Jacob, Chief of Staff of the Eastern Command, arrived by air from Calcutta at 1.20 pm and at once began discussions with General Niazi. An Indian battalion had already entered the city unopposed during the morning, and was joined in the afternoon by four more, including two battalions of the Mukti Bahini. They were greeted in the streets by thousands of jubilant Bengalis, who hugged and kissed the soldiers and garlanded them with flowers.

The surrender terms agreed between General Niazi and General Jacob provided that all Pakistani regular, paramilitary and civilian armed forces would be treated in accordance with the Geneva Convention and that foreign nationals, ethnic minorities and personnel of West Pakistani origin would be protected. After they had been accepted and initialed General Aurora flew to Dacca, accompanied by the Navy and Air Force commanders and the Mukti Bahini Chief of Staff (Group Captain Khondkar, later Ambassador to India). General Niazi signed the surrender documents and presented them to General Aurora at a ceremony at the Dacca Race Course at 4.31 pm while Indian troops held back the cheering crowds.

The text of the instrument of surrender signed by General Aurora and General Niazi is reproduced below:

INSTRUMENT OF SURRENDER

The PAKISTAN Eastern Command agrees to surrender all PAKISTAN Armed Forces in Bangladesh to Lieut General JAGJIT SINGH AURORA, G.O.C. of the Indian and Bangladesh forces in the Eastern Theatre. This surrender includes all PAKISTAN land, air and naval forces as also all paramilitary forces and civil armed forces. These forces will lay down their arms and surrender at the place where they are currently located to the nearest regular troops in the command of Lieut General JAGJIT SINGH AURORA..

The PAKISTAN Eastern Command shall come under the orders of Lieut General JAGJIT SINGH AURORA as soon as this instrument has been signed. Disobedience of orders will be regarded as a breach of the surrender terms and will be dealt with in accordance with the accepted laws and usages of war. The decision of Lieut General JAGJIT SINGH AURORA shall be final should any doubt arise as to the meaning or interpretation of the surrender terms.

Lieut General JAGJIT SINGH AURORA gives his solemn assurance that personnel who surrender shall be treated with the dignity and respect that soldiers are entitled to in accordance with the provisions of the Geneva Convention, and guarantees the safety and well-being of all PAKISTAN military and paramilitary forces who surrender. Protection will be provided to foreign nationals, ethnic minorities and personnel of the West Pakistan region by the forces in the command of Lieut General JAGJIT SINGH AURORA."

The Toll

The Pakistani Ministry of Defence reported on 29 February 1972 fewer than 10,000 of their officers and men were killed or wounded as compared to 30,000 of the enemy. The statement made no reference to those missing or taken prisoner and did not specify what "enemy" meant or whether it included the Mukti Bahini. Revised Indian figures of Indian casualties were given as 3,241 killed (1,765 in West and 1,476 in East), 8,561 wounded and

302 missing and 504 taken prisoner.

The exchange of prisoners who were held in prisoner-of-war camps all over India including Agra, commenced in 1971 but a number who were cited by Bangladesh as liable for war crimes were held back. The exchange of prisoners and repatriation of the Bengalis in Pakistan and non-Bengalis in Bangladesh began on 19 September 1973. This delay occurred because there was heated argument on how to deal with Pakistani prisoners in India charged with war crimes and 203 Bengalis in Pakistan charged with subversion, which subject will possibly afford a story of its own.

The Indian Navy had lost a major ship, INS Khukri and one aircraft. Its toll was some 20 officers and 200 men. The Pakistan Navy in its surrender in the East saw 97 officers and 1,312 sailors taken as prisoners of war which included 3 Captains and 12 Commanders.

Who Started the War?

The subject has been argued between India and Pakistan, fired by accusations by USA that it was India that precipitated the war.

India that precipitated the war. The fact that Mrs. Gandhi was away in Calcutta, Jagjivan Ram, the Defence Minister in Patna enroute to Bangalore, and the Finance Minister away in Bombay on 3 December will explain that the Government of India was caught off guard. In this connection, Mrs. Gandhi wrote to President Nixon one 15 December:

I am writing at a moment of deep anguish at the unhappy turn which the relations of our two countries have taken. I am setting aside all pride, prejudice and passion, and trying as calmly as I can, to analyse once again the origins of the l tragedy which is being enacted. There are moments in history when brooding tragedy and its dark shadows can be lightened by recalling great moments, of the past. One such great moment which has inspired millions of people to die for liberty was the declaration of independence by the United States of America. That declaration stated that whenever any form of government becomes destructive of man's inalienable rights to life, liberty and the pursuit of happiness, it is the right of the people to alter or abolish it.

All unprejudiced persons objectively surveying the grim events in Bangladesh since March 25 have recognised the revolt of 750,000,000 people, a people who were forced to the conclusion that neither their life nor their liberty, to say nothing of the possibility of pursuit of happiness, was available to them. The world Press, radio and television have faithfully recorded they story. The most perceptive of American scholars who are knowledgeable about the affairs of this subcontinent revealed the anatomy of East Bengal's frustrations.

The tragic war which is continuing could have been averted if during the nine months prior to the Pakistani attack on us. On December 3, the great leaders of the world had paid some attention to the fact of the revolt, had tried to see the reality of the situation and searched for a genuine basis for reconciliation. I wrote letters along these lines. I undertook a tour in quest of peace at a time when it was extremely difficult to leave the country, in the hope of presenting to some of the leaders of the world, what the situation was. There was sympathy and support for refugees, but the disease itself was ignored.

War could also have been avoided if the power, influence and authority of all States, and above all of the United States, had got Sheikh Mujibur Rahman released. Instead we were told that a civilian Administration was being installed. Everyone knows that this civilian Administration was a farce. Today, farce has turned into tragedy. Lip service was paid to the need for a political solution, but not a single worthwhile step was taken to bring this about. Instead, Rulers of West Pakistan went ahead holding farcical elections to seats which had been arbitrarily declared vacant..

There was not even a whisper that any one from the outside world had tried to have contact with Mujibur Rahman. Our earnest pleas that Sheikh Mujibur Rahman should be released or that, even if he were to be kept under detention, contact with him might be established, were not considered practical, on the ground that the USA could not urge policies which might lead to the overthrow of President Yahya Khan. While the United States recognized that Mujib was a core factor in the situation and that unquestionably in the long run Pakistan must acquiesce in the direction of greater autonomy for East Pakistan, arguments were advanced to demonstrate the fragility of the situation and of Yahya Khan's difficulty. Mr President, may I ask you in all sincerity, was the release or even secret negotiations with a single human being, namely, Sheikh Mujibur Rahman, more disastrous than the waging of war.

The fact of the matter is that the rulers of West Pakistan got away with the impression that they could do what they liked, because no one, not even the United States would choose to take a public position that, while Pakistan's integrity was certainly sacrosanct, human rights and liberty were no less so, and that there was a necessary interconnection between the inviolability of States and the contentment of their people.

Despite continued defiance by the rulers of Pakistan of the most elementary facts of life, we would still have tried our hardest to restrain the mounting pressure, as we had for nine long months, and war could have been prevented had the rulers of Pakistan not launched a massive attack on us by bombing our airfields in Amritsar, Pathankot, Srinagar, Avantipur, Uttarlai, Jodhpur, Ambala and Agra in broad day light on December 3, at an time when I was away in Calcutta; my colleague, the Defence Minister was in Patna and was due to leave for Bangalore in the South, and another senior colleague of mine, the Finance Minister, was in Bombay. The fact that this initiative was taken at this particular time of our absence from the capital showed perfidious intentions. In the face of this, could we simply sit back trusting that the rulers of Pakistan or those who were advising them had peaceful, constructive and reasonable intent?

We are asked what we want. We seek nothing for ourselves. We do not want any territory of what was East Pakistan and now constitutes Bangladesh. We do not want any territory of West Pakistan. We do want lasting peace with Pakistan. 'But will Pakistan give up its ceaseless and yet pointless agitation of the last 24 years over Kashmir?

Are they willing to give up their hate campaign and posture of perpetual hostility towards India? How many times in the last 24 years have my father and I offered a pact of non-aggression to Pakistan? It is a matter of recorded history that each time such an offer was made, Pakistan rejected it out of hand.

We are deeply hurt by innuendoes and insinuations that it was we who have precipitated the crisis, or in any way thwarted or hindered a solution. During my visits to the United States, the United Kingdom, France, Germany, Austria and Belgium the point I emphasised, publicly as well as privately was the immediate need for a political settlement. We waited nine months for it. When Dr. Kissinger came in August 1971 1 had emphasised to him the importance of seeking an early political settlement. But we have not received even to this day the barest framework of a settlement which would take into account the facts as they are and not as they imagine them to be. .

Be that as it may, it is my earnest and sincere hope that with all the knowledge and deep understanding of human affairs you, as President of the "United States and reflecting the will, the aspirations and idealism of the great American people, will at least let me know where precisely we have gone wrong before your representatives or spokesmen deal with us with such harshness of language.

An official Indian spokesman confirmed on 20 December that Mrs. Gandhi had received a reply from President Nixon, but declined to disclose its contents. The situation today with Mrs Gandhi's son Rajiv in the driving seat opens vistas for thought and dialogue with USA, almost in the same climate that Mrs. Gandhi had to face.

General Musa's Views

The die is now cast. In his book Jawan to General Gen Mohammed Musa HJ (ABC Publishing House, New Delhi) chides Gen Yahya Khan for the war. His argument is both logical and revealing. The author proves that on 21 November 1971 which is an interesting date (it was also a day of Id and joy), Indian troops crossed the border into 'East Pakistan. He writes:

The tried and tested strategic concept and defence of East Pakistan lay in West Pakistan, was forgotten and instead of launching a massive counter offensive from West Pakistan after India invaded the Eastern wing, no action was taken from the Western wing for 12 crucial days. It was not till 3 December 71 that retaliation from West Pakistan was started with an air strike on some enemy air bases followed by what amounted to only a show of force along the border a except three relatively minor attacks against Poonch, Chhamb and Ramgarh in Rajasthan out of which ultimately only the Chhamb Operation was successful.

If nothing else, this puts the lid on the issue of who started the 1971 war. The logical explanation is clear. India did covertly support the war effort in East Bengal but did not start the War with Pakistan. Skirmishes in end-November did anger Indian armed forces to cross the international border to show the Pakistan Army in East Bengal that the Indian Army would not tolerate nonsense and maintain a supine posture. Therefore, it is reasonable to accept and quote General Musa from his autobiography:

On 21 November, without a formal declaration of war, as in 1965, Indian armed forces crossed the international borders in East Pakistan and launched full-fledged attacks from four directions—north, east, west, and north-west. It was Eid day. The planners in GHQ India and HQ Indian Eastern Command, were probably convinced that the Pakistani soldiers, tired after fighting for eight months, perhaps weakened after fasting for one month, would be easy prey. But it was a miscalculation. Far from being a walk-over, these Ghazis of Islam fought like hungry and wounded tigers. Almost every fighting man was worthy of a Nishan-e-Haider. It goes to the credit of the brave, simple, frugal, undemanding Pakistani -fighting men and their equally brave junior leadership that, in spite of adverse conditions, unfavourable relative strengths, and unfavourable troops to terrain ratio, no infantry battalion locality could be overrun by India. With superior ground and air mobility and the invaluable support of the local population which by then had turned hostile to Pakistan, India's land and air forces were able to outflank Pakistani units and formations. But infantry battalions had to be launched to capture Pakistan army platoon localities, brigades to capture company localities and in the process Indian army units suffered heavy casualties. Our high command seemed to have been obsessed with defending the border areas, and lacking compatible mobility, formations could not fall back in time and strength on to Dacca and Chittagong areas which should have been defended as fortresses.

What should have been a ceasefire in the East and West Pakistan was turned into a surrender in East Pakistan mainly due to internal and international intrigues and manipulations. As leader of the Pakistan delegation to the UN, Bhutto tore up the cease-fire resolution, walked out, feigned illness, and did not attend the UN debate till Dacca was about to fall. He thus created conditions in which our armed forces had to surrender and face captivity for over two years when a ceasefire could have been arranged, and the handing over of our valiant boys as prisoners of war for so long could have been avoided. Or was it deliberately done to prevent early repatriation of these angry young men who would have come home to take the guilty 'leaders' to task for their complicity in the machinations within the country and those instigated by external agencies for the top-level capitulation? Even after two years of captivity, when these dauntless officers and men came back, still with fire in them, many were discharged or released, their parent units not initially re-raised, and many were launched into Baluchistan to cool them off. We thus lost some of the best combat tested men from 30 odd battalions—any army's valuable asset that just cannot be replaced.

The post-war assertions that West Pakistan was saved from Indian onslaught after the fall of East Pakistan by the intervention of Super or Semi-Super powers are all humbug, Neither the Indian fighting record nor their performance in 1971 in both wings can substantiate either such a capability or likelihood of fulfilling such an intention, even with the help of their new-found friends. Any effort at deep penetration into West Pakistan would have been fully resisted as a people's war by our nation. Let there be no miscalculations on this account in any quarters across our borders.

The 1971 conflict and fall of Dacca was a traumatic experience for all true Pakistanis whether in Pakistan or abroad, and for Pakistan's friends and well-wishers. It produced both grief and anger; it also kindled new determination in the nation.

CAUSES OF PAKISTAN'S DEFEAT

Pakistan claimed it was not defeated: it was humiliated which is worse, as stated by Maj Gen Fazal Muqeem Khan, an ASC Officer, in his book Pakistan's Crisis in Leadership. He asserts that the colonial roots of afsariat (bureaucracy), daftariat (red-tapism) and choudriat (bossism), were the attributes of defeat; but it was lack of a war aim and the political conditions in the East that caused them defeat.

The reaction of Pakistani jawans when ordered to ceasefire was typical. They wept. Havaldar Mohammad Khan aptly summed up the mood in the Punjabi saying "Grandma first made the mistake of getting married, but she' made an even worse mistake by seeking a divorce."

Pakistan launched into war without any national aim. It fought without purpose with total lack of coordination between the civil effort and the armed forces and between the three Services. The Indian victory, Pakistan admits, was due to careful planning and 'a clear national aim.

Gen Fazal Khan goes on to indict Gen Abdul Hamid Khan'(COS) as an indecisive man deep in intrigue against Lt General Peerzada, the PSO to the President whom he very much wanted to be replaced by Maj Gen Ghulam Umar Khan; The Services and especially the Navy were "victims of defection and treachery by the East Pakistanis. Secret plans possibly were leaked, naval dispositions indicated, and the Pakistani Services of a large chunk of good Bengali technicians. Pakistan was hurled into a war they could not win.

Though on 23 November 1971, an Emergency was declared in Pakistan and it was assumed by them that India had attacked East Pakistan in some form, President Yahya Khan let down his military. From the evidence available, it appears that though Gen Yahya Khan had openly declared that an attack on East Pakistan would mean immediate retaliation, he was mentally unable to accept the war he had started. According to the then Commander-in-Chief, Pakistan Navy, Vice Admiral Muzzaffar Hasan, the President's appreciation was that there would be no war. Many claim that Yahya Khan's hesitation over 13 days (21 November to 3 December) caused Pakistan's defeat in the war that followed.

In the Combat (Paris, 27 December 1971) Geoyes Anderson listed the causes for Pakistan's. defeat as follows:

On one point at-least the international strategical experts were not mistaken: they all predicted that the Indo-Pakistani conflict would be short lived and would not last more than three weeks. Most of them were nevertheless surprised by the speed of the defeat and collapse of the Pakistani army, which the Pentagon and a certain number of European Generals considered to be the best in the Asian continent.

However, this is not the first mistake of judgement the U.S. intelligence services have made.

If India was able to win in a fortnight, it was not due only to her superiority in number of troops and in firepower. Among the determining factors on the Indian side were her more detailed planning, better strategical and tactical organization, faultless co-operation of the three arms, readiness to adopt new strategical methods suggested by Soviet Advisers, and last but not least the discipline of her troops and their total confidence in their High Command.

Even before the outbreak of hostilities, Delhi had prepared for the campaign by organizing if not by arming the Mukti Bahini of Bangladesh, who harassed unceasingly the Pakistani occupation forces and contributed notably in destroying their strong points, sapping their morale and interfering with their supplies, in particular by sabotaging their arms and petrol depots. Islamabad's disorganization was aggravated certainly by the disputes and controversies between President Yahya Khan and General Pirzada and Hamid Khan on the one hand and the Ministers, led by Mr. Zulfikar Ali Bhutto on the other; but the most serious was that the fate of the Pakistani Army was entrusted to a pretentious and incompetent General Staff.

The operations were directed by two Generals whose only claim to distinction was their friendship with the A Head of State. The first was General Tikka Khan, Commander of -the Kashmir sector, already notorious on account of massacring "administered" populations which earned him the name of "butcher of Baluchistan and Bengal". As for his military qualifications,' it may be worth recalling that when he was promoted to Lieutenant Colonel, a "confidential" report by his superior officer to General Staff in Karachi stated that "this officer has shown himself unfit to hold posts of high responsibility", The second right hand man of Yahya Khan, General Niazi, although nicknamed by his subordinates. "The Tiger", did not show more strategic ability than his friend Tikka. Brutal, cruel, stupid, boosted up succeed General Tikka Khan as Commander in East "Bengal, he encouraged his men to atrocities and looting to "subdue" the hostile people of the Eastern province. Against these officers, who discredited the Pakistani army, the Indian forces were commanded' by General Jagjit Singh Aurora, whose tactical devices and inspirations took the enemy by surprise, bewildered and routed him.

Pakistan Air Force

As admitted by Pakistan, Pakistan Air Force flew a total of 157 day and 134 night sorties against targets in India in two weeks in the West. In addition, it made 922 sorties in support of Pakistan Army operations and only 27 sorties in support of the Pakistan Navy. It claimed 76 aircraft destroyed (24 SU-7s, 23 Hunters, 10 Canberras, 8 MiG-2l's, 5 HF-24s, 3

Gnats and 3 Mysteres). The claim and the real tally of 42 indicates that Pakistan Air Force was numerically inferior, possessed limitations in radar cover but the individual pilots and technical support were of a high standard. Centralised direction to PAF has been attributed as the cause for not doing better. The Pakistan Air Force claims they were deployed too thinly and deeply. Centralised control kept them on a leash. As for inter Service Co-operation, it had not acquired any maritime support and could not give the Navy meaningful support. The support to the Army was plentiful but lacked co-ordination.

Indian Navy's Success

The brilliant planning and attention to principles of war in embarking upon bold operations was the prime cause of the Indian Navy's superior performance... The Chief of Naval Staff, Admiral SM Nanda's lines of communication and his inquiring mind were forever open and ticking. One is reminded of how as Chief of Naval Staff, he once visited Bombay and in a restaurant called "Bullock Cart" near "Lion's Gate, saw a few young naval couples having a meal. He or invited all the young wives to his VIP table for an aperitif and simply asked them "What is wrong with the Navy at Bombay?" After some coaxing they opened up, they complained of ration collection from Colaba, ASC depot, housing and such Service related matters. Next he asked what ailed their husbands; and another list emerged. The next day armed with this information he posed the-same question in Western Naval Command Office to -the Commander-in-Chief. When the local parish Admiral attempted to say all seemed well, Nanda in his booming voice described his previous night's brain-storming session and told the local C-in-C what shortcomings there were in his very command. Most were remedied and answers to others were found. The same technique of open line communication was used by Nanda in the 1971 war to seek a motivated and co-operative effort.

He made his operational Commanders-in-Chief do an appreciation and made his Director of Naval Operations Dawson, the then Captain at Naval Headquarters and later Chief of Naval Staff do likewise. In fact in 1974, the Royal Naval Staff College, London taught this technique and called it the tri-appreciation and gave credits to Nanda because he is known to have taken the various appreciations and then extrapolated and dictated what he thought were to be the Indian Navy's operational tasks. He dictated the Operations orders to a confidant of his and sealed them up for he was unsure of unintentional leaks by his own staff. Meetings with Admirals Krishnan and Kohli meant long sessions clearing his mind on actual capabilities of ships and at times he had no hesitation to differ with his Vice Chief and Director of Naval Operations where he felt it fit. Thus the final operation orders were reframed. This prime activity set the ball rolling for clear-cut directives and the attacks on Karachi were a direct result.

Use of INS Vikrant by Krishnan who knew the ship he had earlier commanded and dedication by officers and men over and above the call of duty were hallmarks which led to successes in the East, soon after the only possible major threat there PNS Ghazi lay silent at the bottom of the sea at the doorstep of Visakhapatnam. The fleet contributed what it could, but failed to foray into Karachi till 9 December and it was the small Banana boats (banana, because jokingly, the Osa-class boats are supposedly paid for by exports to USSR, then bananas in plenty), which later came to be called Killers showed that Karachi was not impregnable. Intelligence to locate the Pakistan Navy Fleet ships failed, and as one later learnt they had stayed near Churna Island off Karachi. This fact kept the Indian Navy's Western Fleet guessing and they began to concentrate on merchant ship interceptions, till guided by their Commander-in-Chief and Naval Headquarters.

Much time was lost. Yet the blockade was complete and the Indian Navy's successes were well appreciated by the nation and its leaders.

In concluding this account of the exploits of the Indian Navy in the 1971 war, it may be well to cite the exploits of the Pakistan navy as seen by one of their own men.

PAKISTAN NAVY IN THE WAR
Maj. Gen. Fazal Muqueem Khan

The story of the Navy is a story of Continuous struggle to establish its role and attain its rightful place in the defence hierarchy of Pakistan. The importance of maritime power was never appreciated adequately and little could be spared from the expenditures on the Army and the Air Force to provide for the Navy. A low priority to the Navy was perhaps, natural, as the men who had the overriding say in defence matters had inherited
ta long and distinguished tradition of soldiering and had all been soldiers. For them, the sea was remote. Under colonial rule, the British Royal Navy guarded India's sea frontiers as part of its imperial responsibility. There was no need to keep an Indian 'fleet in being'. Small anti-gun running squadron at the Indian station was all that was necessary as an auxiliary to the strategically mobile British Royal Navy. On the other hand, a large standing army was created in India for internal security, to safeguard the land frontiers and as a fire brigade for overseas expeditions in imperial interest. The British Indian Army's influence in the Government of India was always pervasive and at times decisive. The Pakistani statesmen and soldiers took to this tradition Without understanding all the implications of governing a sovereign state, unique in its geography and under constant threat from the country, separating the two wings of Pakistan.

Thus the maritime needs of the country separated by 3000 miles of hostile seas were never fully recognised. The location of the Naval Headquarters in Karachi, and the absence of an influential joint planning staff kept the pace of naval development disproportionately slow. With the passage of time the shape and size of the Navy and its very obsolescence ceased to give the Service an image of credibility to fulfil its mission in a war of aggression.

Nevertheless it cannot be over-emphasised that the story of the Navy, in spite of all the discouraging aspects, is a story of long vigil, of great hazards, of gallant deeds in peace and war. Officers and men served their country with the highest devotion, and went about their business without seeking plaudits or applause. Navy traditionally is called the 'Silent Service'.

As a consequence of complete belief in a continental type of strategy, which was continuously opposed by the Navy, the defence thinking against the threat from India relied on a possible of was of short duration which could be waged on stockpiles of arms and ammunition. The main battles of survival, it was thought would be the plains of the' Punjab, and therefore all effort had to be made to strengthen the land/air capability. This precluded any significant role by the Navy to keep the sea lanes open for supplies by sea into East or West Pakistan, or any communications by sea between the two wings of the country during emergencies. The strategy of 'Defence of the East lies in West', unfortunately "even precluded due attention being paid to the local requirements of East Pakistan for riverine warfare which was unavoidable in that area in the event of hostilities.

Between 1947-54, the only naval additions were three British destroyers of World War II which were already obsolescent. By the latter date US military aid had started trickling into the country and in away the Americans became responsible for expanding the Navy a little. Only the US Military Aid Advisory Group's professional opinion which backed the Navy, was able to convince, the then Prime Minister of the need to strengthen the Navy. One second-hand cruiser and five old destroyers were acquired from the United Kingdom in 1955, 1956 and 1957. Even these old vessels could not be modernised due to paucity of foreign exchange. Eighteen months later, Field Marshal Ayub Khan on becoming President, actually ordered a reduction in the size of the Navy. The then C-in-C Navy, Admiral H.M.S Chaudhary protested, and was later retired for his professional disagreement. The courageous step taken by him went completely unnoticed and unlamented by the public, as it was not allowed to be publicised. No new or additional units were added to the Navy between 1957 and 1966 except for one Fleet Oiler and one World War II submarine which was given on loan by the USA, as part of the Aid Programme.

Under the circumstances the role of the Navy during the Indo-Pak War in September 1965 was merely the seaward defence of Karachi, Chittagong and Chalna, and assistance to the Army in the riverine defence of East Pakistan. It was required to carry out only limited escorting of those merchant ships which were bringing in important supplies. In the short duration of the 1965 war, the Navy's performance was much greater than the role demanded and beyond the expectations of the most optimists. It seemed that the Indian Navy was taken completely by surprised and India was unprepared to seek an engagement at sea with a much weaker opponent.

After the 1965 war, the Indian Navy had started expanding at a very fast pace and in a short space of time acquired new frigates, submarines, maritime aircraft, anti-submarine helicopters and missile boats. In addition, large investments were made to improve the naval infrastructure like dockyards, docks, shipways. By 1970, their naval budget was nearly 200 crore rupees with a substantial foreign exchange component. As a matter of comparison the increase in the Indian Navy during the five years after the 1965 War was more than the total strength of the Pakistan Navy quantitatively and many times more qualitatively. The Indians openly embarked on creating two fleets, one for the Bay of Bengal and the other for the Arabian Sea. They had also built a strong naval base in the Andamans for a blockade of East Pakistan. Their Western Fleet could with ease out match the Pakistan Navy in the Arabian Sea and their Eastern Fleet could independently blockade the ports of East Pakistan and prevent supplies from getting into Chittagong or Chalna. On the contrary Pakistan Navy's budget remained around 20 crore rupees with only 4 to 5 crore worth of foreign exchange component. This sum was hardly enough to pay the annual instalments for the-Daphne-class submarines, three of which had been purchased from France in the meantime. No money was, therefore, available for any modernisation, replacement of old ships or acquisition of new equipment. Except for the three recently acquired Daphne-class submarines, Pakistan's main fleet was aging fast. All its other units - one cruiser, seven destroyers and the submarine Ghazi were of World War II vintage and were long past their useful life. Their sea going and fighting capability was quite unsatisfactory. Out of these PNS Tughril, a destroyer, was already on its way to the breaker's yard and the mishap that befell PNS Badr, another destroyer, about the middle of August 1971 created the misapprehensions that most of the other units of the fleet Would soon meet the same fate as PNS Tughril. On August 10, PNS Badr on her passage to Karachi from East Pakistan, met cyclonic weather off the Indian Port of Goa, about 800 miles from its destination. The rough weather was purely seasonal – monsoonic - which a destroyer is built to ride through. As it happened its steel plates were ruptured and a large portion of her bow was lost due to structural weakness resulting from old age. The ship's company, with commendable effort, were successful in their endeavours to control the damage and save the ship. This was a pointer which put the sea-worthiness of the Navy's Surface ships in doubt, let alone the fighting potential.. In the meantime, PNS Alamgir, another destroyer had also developed serious mechanical defects. Three destroyers had, therefore, been demilitarised and the others were equally suspect, creating an understandable demoralizing effect on the ships' companies.

Over and above this the Navy suffered from another great-and telling handicap. It had no maritime air element. Without such a support in modern times, a navy remains blind and helpless. In consequence, the Navy lost a great deal of its offensive and defensive capability. This deficiency of maritime aircraft became more acute because of two new factors. First, with the introduction of Submarines in the Navy, maritime air reconnaissance had become essential for the utilisation of their offensive capability to the full. By nature submarines are slow craft and cannot therefore reconnoitre their targets. They have to be put on to targets. Secondly without assistance of maritime reconnaissance aircraft, the Navy remained completely blind against the operation of Indian missile boats, which had newly been acquired from Russia. According to experts, surface ships are no match for these boats which are small in size with low free-board and therefore difficult to detect. On the other hand they can detect surface ships from about 30 miles without being themselves detected from that distance. A destroyer, could only pick them up from about 10 miles. At the same time they carry deadly weapons which can be fired with effect from about 20 miles and apply their own radar-homing system. In the absence of any other satisfactory defence against them they could only be dealt with by air strikes at their base or at sea. Aircraft were therefore the only means to deal with them. As Pakistan could not a separate naval air force, the Pakistan Air Force was urged the Joint Chiefs Committee at different times since 1963 to purchase maritime reconnaissance and strike aircraft to support the Navy. But no such aircraft had been acquired as maritime air support was a low priority with the PAF; incidentally another indicator of the bankruptcy of coordination in the machinery for the higher direction of war. On the other hand as a result of their experience in 1965, the Indians were fully prepared in 1971. They had taken pains to build up anti—submarine capability and had acquired five anti-submarine frigates from Russia and four most up-to-date anti—submarine helicopters (Sea Kings) from Britain. They had also built up maritime reconnaissance to counter submarines. In short the Navy was forced to go to war with inadequate and outmoded ships and equipment, and without air cover and great quantitative and qualitative disparities. Whereas in the other two sister services, the Army and the Air Force, some expansion had. taken place after the 1965 war, the Navy had to face substantial diminution in its strength. In 1971, it had only 8,000 officers and men, half of them working on shore and the other half at sea. Out of the total strength, 3,000 officers and men belonged to East Pakistan and after military action in that province in March 1971 they became ineffective. This meant that almost overnight the Navy was further reduced in trained manpower by about 38 per cent. Also, at the start of military action in East Pakistan, the Navy was drawn into supporting the Army and the civil administration. The meagre strength of the Navy .in East Pakistan had gradually to be augmented by reducing dangerously the units and installations in West Pakistan. This meant the loss of a large number of experienced and key personnel for non—naval duties in East Pakistan.

The Navy had neither been consulted nor in any way associated with the decision to take military action in East Pakistan. The 'C-in-C Navy had learnt about it only through a chance remark by the President on the midnight of March 25 at Karachi airport, where the C-in-C had gone to receive the President on his return from Dacca. However, Chief of Staff, Navy who had arrived in Dacca in the afternoon of March 25, 1971 after a routine visit to the Chittagong naval base, had been informed of the intended action about a couple of hours before it actually started. He could not contact Chittagong as the telephone lines had been cut. However, due to paucity of troops and the confused situation in Chittagong, the Navy had taken the initiative and secured the airfield on March 26, 1971.

The Navy was thus immediately brought in to support the Army and the civil administration and the tasks allotted to it were briefly as follows:

(a) Supporting the Army in clearing certain rebel strong points along the coast and along the river routes

(b) Restoration of the demolished and paralysed port facilities at Chittagong and Chalna for the even flow of defence stores and civil supplies.

(c) Movement of defence stores and personnel and essential civil supplies up-river by rivers. The road and rail communications had already been badly damaged or become unreliable.

(d) Restoration of the working of the Oil Refinery and the foodgrain silos at Chittagong, both of which had been put out of commission.

On March 25, 1971, the naval units stationed in East Pakistan comprised a» destroyer, the fleet oiler and four patrol craft. Despite its meagre resources in men-and material, the Navy undertook these tasks in a most vigorous manner. It, promptly set out to adopt additional measures to perform satisfactorily the tasks allotted to it. The Army Riverine Support Unit had been lying immobilized due to mechanical defects and non-availability of crews. The unit was reactivated and its LCTs (Landing Craft Tanks) and tugs were manned by the Navy which also provided river pilots as the local pilots had disappeared. This unit under a-naval captain was attached to the Army Logistics Area. The Inland Water Transport Authority and its fleet of rivercraft and coaster had come to a virtual standstill. Its ferries, barges and other craft had been abandoned in remote khals (channels) by the Bengali crew who had fled. The Navy recovered the abandoned craft, repaired them where required and reactivated them. The Inland Water Transport Authority and the East Pakistan Shipping Corporation were once again put on their feet. Naval personnel were provided to man coasters and craft along with civilian crew, engines and other machinery was repaired where necessary and regular services were resumed. Later when rebel activity increased, the coasters were armed and moved under escort provided by gunboats. The Navy also arranged the purchase of more coasters for the movement of food grains and thus helped to avert famine in East Pakistan.

Experienced personnel were also attached to the staff of Headquarters Martial Law to co-ordinate the work of various sea and inland transport agencies. In addition the Navy helped in coordinating the inter-wing and foreign import and export trade. Besides providing gun boat support for certain Army operations, the Navy also raised a marine battalion for riverine operation and ground defence of port installations, which was operative by the beginning of November 1971.

Just before the military action started, the oil refinery in Chittagong had been closed down for routine overhaul and most of its machinery was opened up. Almost all the labour had disappeared on March 26, 1971. In order to meet the increased defence requirements and to keep the duty line of the Province going, it became necessary to reactivate the oil refinery. The Navy made the arrangements to get workmen and technicians from Karachi and soon got it functioning.

Another strange task undertaken by the Navy was to put in commission the damaged grain silos and jetties in Chittagong and Chalna. This was any essential step to avert an impending famine in the province which was looming large owing to the disruption of road and rail' communications caused by insurgents and due to delays in the clearance of cargo from the two ports. The Navy's engineers handled this project with exemplary efficiency and speed.

During this time the Navy had also to clear mines from the water approaches to Chalna port and deal with the activities there. Mining of Chalna port had come as a complete surprise at that time. It was only discovered later that an East German merchant ship while coming out of the port had mined the approaches to it.

The Navy's timely actions and ungrudging assistance in all these vast and important fields not only helped the Army operations but also assisted in restoring normal life and particularly averting the famine which had been forecast by a number of experts.

When the Indian invasion of East Pakistan started on November 21., 1971 Pakistan naval force there was grossly out-numbered by the Indian Eastern Fleet. The destroyer had already been withdrawn earlier to West Pakistan for refit and routine repairs. Starting with four gun boats in the month of March 1971, Admiral Shariff, the Flag Officer Commanding East Pakistan and his young naval officers had gradually built up the strength of small boats to 24 through improvisation and mobilisation of local resources. They were mostly dispersed all over East Pakistan's major rivers in support of Army operations and civil administration. The Eastern Command had continued pressing the Naval Headquarters for an increase in the naval strength. The Navy had,. however, stretched itself to the maximum and could not augment its fleet in East Pakistan. Therefore, no major naval ship was available there. Out of the 24 boats only the four gun boats could be put to sea; the other 20 were river craft, unsuitable for sea operation. Additionally all these boats were armed with short range weapons, more suitable for anti-smuggling operations than for an anti-warship role. Against this force was poised the Indian Aircraft Carrier Task Force of one carrier and eight destroyers/frigates and their Landing Craft Squadron consisting of three LSTs (Landing Ship Tanks).

Moreover, while the Pakistan units had been living and working under war conditions for about eight months, the Indians were fresh and knew that the only opposition they could expect would be from Pakistan's four gun boats. These little boats however continued fighting valiantly till the end. Throughout the war these units without any air cover were constantly strafed by shore and carrier-borne aircraft and suffered heavy casualties. The detailed story of this most uneven but gallantly fought action will be available only when the prisoners of war, now returned to Pakistan are able to tell it. But it is obvious that the odds of the Pakistan Navy against the Indian Navy in this theatre were worse than those of the Revenge against the Spanish Fleet. Admiral Shariff, the Flag Officer Commanding of East Pakistan, reported the conditions of these units as they existed on December 9, 1971. He said that the attrition rate of gun boats was high due to daily mounting and persistent action of the enemy air. He considered that sixty per cent of the naval strength had been rendered non-operational. However till the end, the Indians, in spite of their air and naval supremacy, could not capture the port of Chittagong from seaward and had to do so by an overland assault from Cox's Bazar.

The Naval Headquarters (NHQ) was completely unaware of the cease-fire negotiations between the Eastern Command and the Indians. The C-in-C Navy learnt about it only when Flag Officer Commanding in East Pakistan informed him and asked for instructions in the early hours of the morning of December 16, 1971. Later the same day, he learnt of the cease-fire through the same source. When he asked for confirmation from the Defence Advisor, the latter showed his inability to deny or confirm the news. The confirmation only came when the Admiral at last managed to contact General Hamid, COS Army, later in the day.

The naval war plans had last been reviewed in March 1971 and were based on limited aim achievable by the available strength and state of the weapons and the equipment that the Navy held. As there had been no changes in the Navy, no need was felt to review or revise them after that date. While planning, the Navy had assumed that it would be given a minimum of one week's notice before the war to redeploy and alert its units at sea. It had also expected that the promised limited air support would be made available within 80 miles of Karachi. As for the Indian intentions, the Navy had visualised that with Osa missile boats and submarines available to the Indians, together with the threat from Pakistan submarines, their Navy would not attempt to attack Pakistani ships by their surface ships unless submarines, missiles and air attacks failed to neutralize the Pakistan Navy. Therefore its plans were based on the appreciation that it had no answer to Indian Navy's missile boats. The surface ships were not to be exposed to this danger until the missile boat threat had been neutralised.

The ships had to remain at sea within the Air Force fighter cover. The submarines however were to be deployed on offensive patrols off the major Indian ports and other focal areas.

Like other major military decisions, the C-in-C Navy had neither been consulted nor associated with any of the deliberations that resulted in the decision to counter-attack from West Pakistan. He was merely called up by COS Army, to Rawalpindi on November 29, 1971, and informed of the President's decision to open hostilities in the West in a few days; He was not given the actual date and time which were to be conveyed to him by C-in-C Air through a mutually agreed code word at the appropriate time.

The mutually agreed code was passed to C-in-C Navy at 1515 hours on December 3, 1971, personally by the C-in-C Air. The commanders concerned were hurriedly collected and given their instructions and signals were despatched to all ships by 1700 hours. The Navy had been deployed in their war stations earlier when Indian belligerent intentions had become clear and on subsequent Indian invasion of East Pakistan on November 21, 1971. Some ships were patrolling 140 miles off Karachi and others 70 miles off the port. This was done for monitoring and checking the incoming ships and suspected craft approaching Karachi. Three Daphne submarines were deployed off the Bombay and Kathiawar coast and the submarine Ghazi was despatched to the Visakhapatnam naval base in the Bay of Bengal. The Ghazi's task was to carry out offensive mine-laying against Visakhapatnam and the other three submarines had to attack Indian warships when ordered.

As brought out earlier in this chapter, the Navy, in the absence of any shore-based radar and maritime reconnaissance aircraft was virtually blind. Therefore the services of a civilian radar were requisitioned and Pakistan International Airlines (PIA) willingly provided a Fokker Friendship flight to operate reconnaissance flights. The PIA plane had its own limitations for the purpose it was being used. Its radar was a weather radar and it had only 7 degree decline which could not see downwards. The civil pilots, however, did an extremely good job of work without any previous training in this particular field.

At about the same time on December 3, when Naval HQ was issuing orders and instructions, the Fokker flying along Kathiawar coast-—PIA air patrols had been started on November 30--reported the sighting of Indian Western Fleet consisting of a cruiser, six destroyers and an oil tanker off the Rann of Kutch coast. It was operating around its forward base at Okha. The Pakistani submarines deployed in the area were not able to attack it as they got their orders to commence their operations late that evening. Indeed the submarines had themselves seen the Indian Fleet proceeding overhead on December 2 but were unable to attack for the same reasons. As an alternative, an air strike was requested by the Navy but it was not available. Thus. by not giving sufficient notice of starting the operations to the Navy, a good opportunity to attack the Indian Western Fleet was missed. The first Indian naval action took place on December 4, 1971.

The Indian Air Force and the Navy seemed to have first class co-ordination. They had already established a Joint Operations Centre in Bombay a few months earlier. Indian naval attacks were always covered by the Indian Air Force by keeping Karachi under air attacks. At 0800 hours, the Indian Air Force started strafing Karachi. Two aircraft flew very low over the harbour and an oil tank in Keamari was hit by rockets. Indian aircraft strafed at intervals for the whole, of the day on December 04. While the air raids were going on, the radar picked up a suspect contact at 2100 hours about 40 miles south of Karachi. It must be mentioned here that the presence of Osa missile boats of Russian origin which had been taken over by the Indians, was known and up to the middle of November 1971, Russian naval personnel were seen on these boats in Bombay harbour. The Russian method of deployment which was followed by these boats was that they operated with submarines which acted as watchdogs and observation posts. The Indian submarines were keeping 60 miles off Karachi and closed up only during the night. The Osa boats had to have the submarines at directing platforms for their operations.

After having been informed about the suspect contact, efforts were made to identify this contact. While this was being pursued, the attack came. At 2330 hours the Indian Air Force attack was still on, When PNS Khyber out on a patrol off Karachi, signalled that it had been hit by an aircraft bomb.

The NHQ was taken aback by this information. They could not believe that an aircraft could do this in the middle of the night. They asked for further information. No reply came from the ship as all communications with it had been lost in the meantime. About the same time HQ PNS Wasim, at Manora, reported having seen big fire glow on the horizon out at sea. A fast patrol boat was at once despatched to investigate. On arriving at the site, it found minesweeper PNS Muhafiz, 40 miles off Karachi, burning. The first person to be picked up by this boat from the water was the Captain of the minesweeper. It only came to light through him that the ship had been hit by missile. No report of the incident had been received from this ship. The Indians had hit the two ships simultaneously. Other survivors were also picked up. On receiving information of the missile hit on PNS Khyber, the boat despatched to pick up its returned without success with the excuse that the weather at sea was very choppy and the survivors picked up from the minesweeper were in a bad way and needed medical attention immediately. All efforts were made to locate the Khyber survivors and 70 of them were rescued the next afternoon after about 18 hours of its sinking, although the search had continued by sea and air for the whole of the day.

At midnight on December 4, the local Air Force Commanding Officer was approached to order an attack on the retreating missile boats. It was calculated that they would take six hours to reach their nearest sanctuary and thus allow enough time for the air to attack them early next morning, but no air strike could be made available. It was known later that after the missile attack the Indian boats instead of retreating south, had sailed westward of Gwadar where they stayed for three days. This fact came to notice by a chance conversation with someone travelling in a Cessna which had flown over Gwadar on December 5. After having seen the pictures of the boats he came out with the information that he had seen two of them near Gwadar.

Anyway the Air Force in Karachi did not react to the Navy's request; therefore, the C-in-C Navy rang up the C-in-C PAF in Rawalpindi at 0400 hours and woke him up. After all sorts of pleading, the answer he obtained was "Well old boy, this happens in war. I am sorry your ships have been sunk. We shall try to do something in the future."

After the missile attack the position of the surface ships at sea became almost untenable, as they had no defence against missiles. On December 7, the Flag Officer Commanding the Flotilla, after consulting his sea-going Commanders, met the C-in-C. He acquainted him with the prevailing situation and suggested a withdrawal of the ships inside the harbour in order to escape a missile attack which was most likely to occur. The ships would of course be more susceptible to air attack there, but could also provide a powerful anti-aircraft threat, 'particularly against a low flying attack. It was therefore decided to withdraw all ships to the harbour on December 8 except for the fleet oil tanker which was fully loaded. It had to stay out because of fire hazard within the harbour by its presence and also that its deep draught restricted her entry into port. The oil tanker Dacca was, therefore, ordered to anchor with the other merchant ships away from the port. The Indian missile boats on their passage from Gwadar to Bombay, attacked the merchant ships outside the anchorage at night on December 8. Gulf Star, flying the Panama flag and the US owned ship Venus Challenger were sunk and Hamratton, a British vessel was severely damaged. Dacca along with three merchant ships, was also hit. Her company valiantly fought the fire and saved the ship after heavy damage had been done. One of the missiles fired by Osa boats flew over Manora and hit the first big steel structure it came across. That was one of the oil tanks at Keamari which started a huge fire in the oil farm. The course followed by this missile was strange, perhaps its homing device had failed. The withdrawal of the naval surface ships into harbour was thus claimed by NHQ as a sound tactical move as otherwise, all the naval units would have been attacked by the missile boats and in all probability most of them sunk. Some officers of the Navy thought that it was a shameful act for the Navy to retreat to the harbour. This withdrawal is however a point on which any verdict is best left to naval experts who would probably be discussing this as a case study for years.

On December 8, air attacks on Karachi had started at 2000 hours. Again the air attacks were well coordinated with the missile attack at 2300 hours. Karachi was kept under air attack till 0200 hours on December 9 to give enough time to these missile boats to get away. The Navy was blamed all along by the public for doing nothing against the constant air attacks on Karachi. But the public did not know that the Navy had neither the means nor the responsibility for the air defence of Karachi. The Navy's presence in the harbor however acted as a deterrent to Indian aircraft. The dockyard was bombed but providentially remained safe. Four Indian aircraft were brought down by the Navy's anti-aircraft guns that night.

In the meantime PNS Babur while operating with other units of the Flotilla off the Makran coast in the evening on December 5, engaged a submarine. Destroyers were immediately despatched to carry out anti-submarine operations. Sonar contact of the submarine was achieved with submarine which had by now submerged, and a number of attacks were carried out with anti-submarine mortars. Later, on basis of the evidence collected, the Navy claimed to have damaged the Indian submarine.

Pakistani submarines were operating in their allotted regions. PNS Ghazi which had sailed towards Visakhapatnam with special instructions, had to reach its destination on November 26, 1971. She was to report on arrival but no word was heard from her. Efforts were made. to contact her but to no avail. The fate of the Ghazi was in jeopardy before December 3: The Indians made certain preposterous claims about the sinking of the Ghazi. However, being loaded with mines, it seems to have met an accident on her passage and exploded. A few foreign papers at that time also reported that some flotsam had been picked up by Indian fishermen and handed over to the Indian Navy, which made up stories about its sinking. PN submarine Hangar, operating off the Kathiawar coast stalked and attacked two Indian Navy frigates at night on December 9. It succeeded in sinking one frigate and damaging another. The Indian admission of the loss of 19 officers and 193 sailors and the rescue of six officers and 93 sailors gave the impression that the second frigate might also have been sunk.

A brief mention must be made of the four sea-going naval patrol boats which were operating in East Pakistan waters. After having operated continuously for about nine months one of them was sunk through enemy air action during the last days of the war. Two of them were scuttled in Chittagong harbour at the time of surrender in East Pakistan. The fourth,

PNS Rajshahi, made a heroic and spectacular escape against great odds and through the heavily mined and extensively patrolled water approaches by the Indian Navy off Chittagong harbour. The Captain of the Rajs/zahi. Lieutenant Sikandar Hayat took the daring step and his gallant crew responded.

The overall losses on both sides which were almost equal were as under:

Units	Pakistan Navy	Indian Navy
Destroyers/frigates	1 Sunk	1 Sunk, 1 Damaged
Submarines	1 Sunk (due to an accident onboard)	1 Damaged
Mine Sweepers	1 Sunk	1 Sunk
Patrol Craft	1 Sunk	3 Sunk
Aircraft	0	11 destroyed by naval guns

The Navy's claims about the sinking of Indian ships -- some acknowledged by Indians-- needed to be highlighted. So far as is known the Indians admitted the sinking of their anti-submarine frigate Khukri. Any professional naval commentator would describe this feat as outstanding, firstly because Pakistan submarines were operating without support aircraft and secondly because the enemy vessel was equipped with all sorts of modern equipment to destroy submarines. Thirdly, the war at sea, particularly the submarine war takes a long time to develop, and this achievement took place within a few days of the start of a very short war. Fourthly, the submarine normally attacks the defenceless merchant ships which cannot retaliate, whereas this was an attack against a man-of-war. After the war, even the critical BBC commentators praised Pakistan's naval effort. Considering the shape and size and age of the ships at its command, they said, the Pakistan Navy had acquitted itself well against the Indian Navy.

Ranjit B. Rai

EPILOGUE : THE FUTURE

War is a severe teacher. With the lessons learnt in the 1971 War Pakistan has gone all out to build up a defence for Karachi. It has built new harbours at Qasim, Gwadar and Pasni; acquired lethal missiles like the Harpoon and the Exocet; and added more ships and submarines to its Fleet. It has revamped its armoured and artillery brigades, and built up a respectable Air Force equipped with radar, missiles and F-16 with ambitions of AWACS aircraft in its arsenal. The Soviet incursion into Afghanistan in 1980 has given it the excuse to ask blatantly for US and Chinese arms aid. Leaning on the plea that the arms are to safeguard its interests on the Afghan border, this aid has been forthcoming in plenty. Tanks, missile boats and nuclear know-how from China coupled with sophisticated aircraft and equipment from USA make Pakistan a force reckon with in hardware. It is generally admitted that Pakistan has armed itself over and above its required capability. But whether, the material alone is the telling factor in a war is a moot point for Indian defence planners. After all, Pakistan still remains a military dictatorship, and that fact remains relevant.

Pakistan's acquisition of military hardware has been done, mainly, with the unstated objective of posing 'a challenge to India all over again. Therefore, though a peace call is in the air in the subcontinent, the factors that led to a war also in Kashmir sparked off by the Bangladesh incident have not changed for India as far as Pakistan is concerned. Pakistan still hangs onto Kashmir and has claims on West Siachen. Thus India still has to divert a fair quantum of its resources to build up its armed forces to safeguard itself against a repeated Pakistani attack. The collusion of Pakistan with USA and China tacitly remains, while India's threads with the Soviet Union still remain strong.

The Naval Scene
A second look at the Jane's Fighting Ships 1986-87 makes for interesting comparison, and is recommended.

I have taken the liberty to briefly write on 'The Future'. In this, I have based several premises on today's lack of respect for international law by nations. The tendency to flout international law has become endemic.

Chronic instability of a government, availability of lethal weapons to knockoff nuclear plants in neighbouring countries, terrorism and sabotage cause sudden crises and skirmishes from which, for fear of nuclear confrontation the superpowers try to steer clear. More recently and after 1971, the Falklands war the continuing Iran-Iraq war and escapades of Israel, Somalia and Libya and USA in Nicaragua give credence to the theory that minor wars will never be avoided but the future manner of battle is likely to change. In the Iran-Iraq war, major cities like Baghdad and Tehran have been spared aerial attack; life goes on undisturbed; yet the two nations wage a severe battle on the borders and at sea. A sense of "controlled battle" during war seems to be emerging. In this context, confrontation at sea has many attractions for an aggressor. Nuclear weapons could also be employed with a greatly reduced risk of retaliation. As Anthony Preston in World War III Naval Review says, "Sad as it is to admit, public opinion would probably accept. the deaths of several hundred sailors in the North Atlantic whereas the threat of nuclear weapons being use on land is likely to produce widespread panic among civil population." This is a pointer to the future. With satellite communications and reconnaissance, and cruise missiles at sea, the scenario is going to be dynamic for those nations who can claim good knowledge and intelligence of the dimensions of space over, under and on the seas. India will have to play its role in the Indian Ocean accordingly. The Indian Navy cannot ever say "Ring of the main engines. Revert to normal notice for steam." It will have to lift its head in the Indian ocean and keep boilers banked if not steaming.

Key Index

China's Role in Bangladesh issue: 1, 7, 9, 10, 13, 16, 23, 24, 38, 46, 48, 50, 51, 52, 70, 78, 80, 84, 89, 136
Cox Bazar: 23,71,76,77,79,80 - 82,85,90,92,95,130
Eastern Fleet: 20,30,35,61,68,76,81-82,90,92,93,101,126,129
Eastern Naval Command: 31,72,75,81,98,99,100
Indian Aircraft Carrier Task Force: 129
Indian Navy's attack of Karachi: 2,18,22,28,29,47,64,73-75,77,83,84,86,93-95,97,98,101,102,121, 123-127,129-134,136
Indian Ocean Super Power Games: 47 - 50, 137
INS Khukri: 19,21,61,70,86,101 - 107,115,135
INS Vikrant: 19-21,23,27 - 30,54,61,62,68,69,71,72,76,79,81,90,93,97 - 99,101,102,108,109,123
Jerath, lt. Cdr Vijay: 22,83,86
Kohli, VADM, S.N: 19,31,61,73,84,122,
Krishnan, Admiral: 19,20,31,69,77,82,90,98 - 100,122,123
Landing Craft Squadron: 128,129
Nanda, Admiral, S.M: 2,18,21,29,31,61,64,74,100,106,122
OSA Class: 26,27,29,70,123,130,132,133
PNS Ghazi: 30,35,61,62,69,72,82,87,94,97 - 101,102,118,123,126,131,134
Royal Navy Task Force: 87
TG 74 (USS Enterprise): 43,49
Western fleet: 18,29,31,61,67,69,73,75,84,93,95,103,123,131
Western Naval Command: i,19,29,31,74,75,105,122

ABOUT THE AUTHOR

CMDE Ranjit Bhawani Rai (Retd.) served in the Indian Navy, commanded four ships and the Naval Academy. He served twice in the NHQ as the Director of Operations and later Intelligence. He also served as Defence Adviser in Singapore. Leaving Navy prematurely, he attended IIM (Ahmedabad) for Shipping Management and was the rep for Waterman Shipping Corp USA (1993-2004), when India liberalized and shipping thrived. After US flagged ships withdrew to war in Iraq, he took to writing, broadcasting, and conferences. Author of four books, his avocations are TV commentary, golf and supporting his wife's inbound tourism activities.

Get Published with Frontier India

Do you want to get your book or thesis published? You might even want to republish your book which is currently out of print.. Frontier India Technology as a publisher, distributor and retailer of books, offers a complete range of publishing, editorial, and marketing services that helps you as an author to take his or her book to the reader.

Getting your work published is a wish for many for reasons including profit earning, self-satisfaction, popularity and other good reasons. We will offer you choices based on your needs. Get in touch with us at frontierindia@gmail.com.

Our Recently Published Books include :

An Indian Air force Recollects by Wing Co P.K. Karayi (Retd.) ISBN: 978-8193005507

Warring Navies – India and Pakistan (International Edition) – by Cmde Ranjit B. Rai (Retd.). Joseph P. Chacko. ISBN: 978-8193005545

Basics of marriage Management by Walter E Vieira. ISBN: 978-8193005514

Beat That Exam Fever – Succeed in Examinations by Walter E Vieira. ISBN: 978-8193005538

Ordinary Stocks, Extra Ordinary Profits by Anand S. ISBN: 978-8193005521

Foxtrot to Arihant – The Story of Indian Navy's Submarine Arm by Joseph P. Chacko. ISBN: 978-8193005552

The Role of the President of India by Prof Balkrishna. ISBN 13: 978-81-930055-6-9

Foxtrots of the Indian Navy by Cmde P.R. Franklin. ISBN 13: 978-81-930055-7-6

Book Republishing Project

A lot of popular books have gone **out of print** and there is a small demand for these books. Frontier India Technology has begun **Re-Publishing** such books.

If you are an author and you have out of print books, we can help you to get it back into the market.

An author has to do three things. 1) get rights back from publisher who is not ready to print it. 2) give us a soft copy or send us a hard copy and we will digitize it for a fee 3) sign an agreement with us.

We will bring the book into market in limited copies. When sold, the author gets a regular 10% on sale.

About Copyrights:
If you are the author of a book that has gone out of print, you may not have the rights to republish it unless your original contract defines what constitutes "out of print" and specified that at that point, the rights revert to you. If your publisher has gone out of business, be prepared to buy the remaining inventory and the rights. In case you are unsure, consult a lawyer.

www.ingramcontent.com/pod-product-compliance
Lightning Source LLC
Chambersburg PA
CBHW060837190426
43197CB00040B/2667